Ready for Kindergarten

T0243468

Other Redleaf Press books by Angèle Sancho Passe

Creating Diversity-Rich Environments for Young Children

Dual-Language Learners: Strategies for Teaching English

Early Childhood Leadership and Program Management

Evaluating and Supporting Early Childhood Teachers

I'm Going to Kindergarten!

READY
for Kindergarten

Second Edition

A Tool Kit
for Supporting
Children and Families

ANGÈLE SANCHO PASSE

Redleaf Press®
www.redleafpress.org
800-423-8309

Published by Redleaf Press
10 Yorkton Court
St. Paul, MN 55117
www.redleafpress.org

© 2010, 2023 by Angèle Sancho Passe

All rights reserved. Unless otherwise noted on a specific page, no portion of this publication may be reproduced or transmitted in any form or by any means, electronic or mechanical, including photocopying, recording, or capturing on any information storage and retrieval system, without permission in writing from the publisher, except by a reviewer, who may quote brief passages in a critical article or review to be printed in a magazine or newspaper, or electronically transmitted on radio, television, or the internet.

First edition 2010
Second edition 2023
Cover design by Jim Handrigan
Cover photo by Fstop123/istockphoto/Getty Images
Interior typeset in Utopia and designed by Douglas Schmitz
Printed in the United States of America
30 29 28 27 26 25 24 23   1 2 3 4 5 6 7 8

Library of Congress Cataloging-in-Publication Data
Names: Passe, Angèle Sancho, author.
Title: Ready for kindergarten : a tool kit for supporting children and
    families / Angèle Sancho Passe.
Other titles: Is everybody ready for kindergarten?
Description: Second edition. | St. Paul, MN : Redleaf Press, 2023. |
    Revised edition of: Is everybody ready for kindergarten? | Includes
    bibliographical references and index. | Summary: "The transition to
    kindergarten is a significant and exciting milestone in young children's
    lives. This tool kit is an ideal planning resource for early childhood
    professionals as they coordinate a successful transition that benefits
    children, their families, and schools"— Provided by publisher.
Identifiers: LCCN 2023011628 (print) | LCCN 2023011629 (ebook) | ISBN
    9781605548005 (paperback) | ISBN 9781605548012 (ebook)
Subjects: LCSH: Kindergarten. | Kindergarten--Parent participation.
Classification: LCC LB1167 .P37 2023 (print) | LCC LB1167 (ebook) | DDC
    372.21/8--dc23/eng/20230403
LC record available at https://lccn.loc.gov/2023011628
LC ebook record available at https://lccn.loc.gov/2023011629

Printed on acid-free paper

To all the children getting ready for kindergarten together with their families and educators

Contents

Acknowledgments

Since 2010, the first edition of this book has generated much interest as I engaged in presentations, workshops, e-learning courses, discussions, and reflections with many early educators: teachers, family child care providers, and administrators. I am grateful for the exchanges and the attention. Large and small school districts, state agencies, foundations, and individual schools and programs have used these ideas to make plans to prepare children and families for the transition to kindergarten. I am honored to have contributed to all these efforts. Thank you, Redleaf Press, for producing version one and, now, for facilitating version two.

Preface to the Second Edition

The title of the first edition of this book was a question: *Is Everybody Ready for Kindergarten?* At the time of the original version, the concept of a deliberate transition to kindergarten was emergent. There was even a debate over who should be "most" ready: children, families, early educators, or schools. Through research and application, the fact has now been established that children do better in kindergarten when they are prepared socially and academically in pre-K. We know as well that when their families are supported, children better know what to expect, and they participate in the preparation. And for all of that to happen, early educators must be knowledgeable and intentional in their practices with children and families. Readiness for kindergarten is not a question anymore. This second edition of the book is therefore an assertion: *Ready for Kindergarten: A Tool Kit for Supporting Children and Families.* The objective is clear: we must follow sound principles of child and family development while using effective educational strategies, such as those presented in this tool kit.

Changes in society and in education over the decade since the first edition of this book have affected children's readiness for kindergarten. Many are positive but some have been disruptive, such as the global COVID-19 pandemic from which we are emerging in 2023, at the time of this writing. During these stressful times, schools and many early education programs were closed, and young children missed out on in-person education in preschool and kindergarten. That resulted in loss of formal learning that worried families and educators (Institute of Education Sciences 2022). Nevertheless, as the crisis resolves, millions of children are making the transition from preschool or home to elementary school, and it is an enriching growth experience.

Beyond the effects of the global health crisis, the Black Lives Matter movement and other happenings have inspired a reckoning on race relations and a heightened awareness of the need for equity in life and in education. The use of technology has grown in all areas of life for adults and children. International instability, financial inflation, and climate change are also making people and communities rethink our approach to the future.

Significantly, early childhood education has been elevated to a topic of everyday conversation since the pandemic highlighted the importance of child care for working families. Widespread challenges in the field have surfaced, including the low pay for child care workers and the worker shortage. This has created new urgency for early childhood professionals and policy makers to improve the condition of early educators and to make significant investments in quality early care and education, specifically for kindergarten readiness, as described in the 2023 Early Care and Education Crisis Work Group Legislative Priorities (2023).

While the community and the field of early childhood education work to problem solve challenges, it is good to take inventory of the positives that have happened in the past decade. There have been massive efforts to increase quality in the classroom and big strides in research on child development and learning, especially in literacy. The training and professional development of educators has grown as a priority. As the leader in the field, the National Association for the Education of Young Children (NAEYC) has shined a light on the imperative to organize as a profession, assembling everyone who educates and cares for children in what is now a widely disorganized system. NAEYC has also continued to explore developmentally appropriate practices, ethics, and equity as it revises position statements and refines its recommendations.

In 2022, the US Department of Education released the *Report on the Condition of Education 2022* (Institute of Education Sciences 2022). It examines the state of education from 2010 to 2021. These items are relevant to our thinking about the preparation for and transition to kindergarten:

- The poverty rate of children is lower than in 2010.
- More children live in households where a parent has completed high school.
- More children live in married-couple households, except for Black children.
- More than 90 percent of children ages three to eighteen have internet access at home through a computer or smartphone.
- The majority of five-year-olds (86 percent) are enrolled in a pre-K program (private, school-based, full-time, or half-time).
- The number of white and Black children enrolled in public schools has decreased since 2009, while the number of Hispanic children enrolled has increased.
- The number of students served by the Individuals with Disabilities Education Act (IDEA) has increased, as has the number of students who are dual-language learners.
- The number of school dropouts has declined since 2010.
- Educational attainment—such as graduation from a high school, a two- or four-year college, or a graduate school—has increased for all races.
- Funding for public education has increased since 2009 in all respects, from facilities to salaries to special services.
- More families report reading to their children three times a week.

The families of today's kindergartners are the most educated in history. The increase in the number of educational toys and books and the availability of parent-child activity programs is apparent everywhere from discount stores to public libraries. The efforts of our field in promoting early literacy, including reading and talking to young children, have permeated society.

NAEYC, the US Department of Education, state agencies, foundations, public school systems, and private education institutions have been increasingly investing in and promoting school readiness. The Quality Rating and Improvement System (QRIS) movement has continued to expand, with forty-four states participating as of 2022. This has driven an increase in quality in the pre-K programs preparing children for kindergarten.

From the objective perspective of the data in the report, the state of early education has improved. We must take heart in the positive news while at the same time continue to do better. Now, as the public health situation improves, enrollment in kindergarten is expected to stabilize. Those of us working on the transition to kindergarten in pre-K programs and services still have the important job to be ready ourselves so we can teach children and support their families well.

Beyond the Pandemic

The COVID-19 pandemic was very difficult for everyone, including young children, their families, and educators. Many children stayed home to avoid contagion and had limited social experiences outside of their immediate family. Early childhood centers used all manner of creativity to offer online services from circle time to early literacy activities. The child care programs that stayed open used stringent health measures such as wearing masks and asking parents to drop off children at the door to minimize contact.

While all these new practices were perturbing, early educators and the children also found opportunities for growth (Passe 2021). The concept of post-traumatic growth comes from the field of positive psychology. It posits that adversity can yield changes in understanding oneself, others, and the world that result in personal growth and increased self-confidence. I certainly get that sense after attending early childhood conferences in 2022 and 2023, as well as when I train pre-K educators and family child care providers in workshops. Educators appear energized and committed to their profession.

It is true that children who missed time in pre-K during the pandemic and are entering kindergarten are likely to need scaffolding so they have the readiness skills expected. As we hear calls for accelerating learning or catching up, we must always remember that the best way to catch up is by focusing on learning through play, using a play-based intentional curriculum, as noted later in this book.

A study of preschool programs in Tennessee demonstrated that children who attend school readiness programs that are not developmentally appropriate do not have any advantage in success in education (Durkin et al. 2022). The research also shows that quality programs that *are* developmentally appropriate increase the literacy and math skills of children (Schmitt et al. 2023).

The kindergartners of the twenty-first century are steeped in literacy, with the most literate families in history. Children have bedsheets with letters and numbers on them, and educational toys and apps abound. They often have "school skills," such as knowing the alphabet, writing their names, and using their parents' tablets. But they are still young children whose brains and bodies need movement, hands-on experiences, and opportunities for learning by doing. They need to learn both academic and social skills to function well in school and society. That means that as educators, we have this amazing chance to support them and their families in the entrance to kindergarten with optimism. The pandemic was a terrible time, but we are moving on with confidence in our teaching skills and caring attitude. The increased attention to the conditions of the field of early childhood education and the prospect of additional funding can also be seen as hopeful signs for the future.

Emerging Trends

The science and art of early childhood education continues to evolve. This evolution can be seen in the work of NAEYC on developmentally appropriate practice between 1986 and 2022. There have been new understandings of cognitive science, with an emphasis on early literacy, numeracy, and STEM (science, technology, engineering, and mathematics). There has also been research on social-emotional learning (SEL) that prompts educators to pay attention to children's social behaviors and executive functioning. I want to touch on some of these trends, as they pertain to the transition to kindergarten.

Technology

The use of technology has skyrocketed both as an instructional tool and as entertainment. Excessive use of technology does affect children's behavior in negative ways. While children appear calm when occupied with a device, they become irritable when pulled from it and act out in frustration. There has been an increase in children misdiagnosed with attention deficit hyperactivity disorder (ADHD), autism, or other disorders and put on medications when the underlying cause is electronic screen syndrome (ESS) (Dunckley 2015). Yet as pre-K educators become aware of the negative effects, they must also be knowledgeable of the positive aspects of technology when used wisely and with intention (Puerling 2018), helping families avoid the pitfalls of technology while enjoying its benefits.

Playful Learning

As the pendulum swings between academics and free play, the term *playful learning* brings clarity to the concept of play-based early education (Zosh et al. 2022). It defines play on a spectrum that is not all teacher-directed nor only child-initiated. It is about coupling a rich curriculum with a playful pedagogy. For example, rather than having children learn letters by rote repetition, they learn them by singing songs, going on a hunt at the sensory table, or making them out of playdough. Through careful planning based on the early learning standards, the teacher's curriculum activities allow children to explore and express themselves at the same time as they make progress toward learning goals.

Social-Emotional Learning (SEL)

Children experience a full range of "big feelings," including anger, fear, happiness, sadness, excitement, and frustration. As with physical and cognitive skills, young children also must develop social-emotional skills. That means they learn about who they are and how to get along with others. They learn how to control their feelings so that when they are upset, they can talk about it instead of screaming. They need the guidance of adults as they learn to calm down, control their impulses, and focus on solutions. To that effect, SEL is an integral part of a preschool and early elementary curriculum, as children practice skills such as self-confidence, empathy, friendship, and responsibility with their classmates in the social environment of the classroom.

Trauma-Informed Care and Education

Trauma-informed care and education is centered around the idea that teaching skills such as executive function, making friends, problem solving, and empathy helps prepare children for school and school success. As such, it is a strength-based approach that focuses on the whole child, not on any trauma itself (Nicholson, Perez, and Kurtz 2019). Trauma-informed care and education is not a therapeutic intervention, and it benefits all children. It asks educators to be mindful of their biases and not make assumptions about what children and families need, and it requires everyone to work together for success. The overall message is to believe in the resilience of children and trust that they can learn emotional regulation and impulse control.

Behavior Guidance

In educators' and parenting forums, the unruly behavior of young children is often a topic of concern. Kindergarten teachers ask that early childhood educators send them well-behaved children who can sit at circle time without picking on their classmates. They say that social skills are more important than knowing all the letters of the alphabet. Yet there are differing views on appropriate behavior and different strategies on how to achieve it. In pre-K classrooms, some reasons for misbehavior may be related to children's personal experiences such as traumas or home-life disruptions. Other reasons may be that educators have negative biases toward certain children or that their own expectations mismatch with reality. Misbehavior might increase because of educators' teaching practices, such as running a classroom that lacks routines, that has an understimulating curriculum, or that has overstimulating clutter such that children cannot make sense of the day or the space. Pre-K educators must pay attention to their environments and their own biases to help decrease behavior issues while they help children practice positive social-emotional skills to prepare for kindergarten.

Diversity and Equity

Recently there has been increased awareness and knowledge of the impact of diversity and equity in teaching and behavior guidance. Behavior guidance is the area of education most vulnerable to educators' biases. Educators are asked to consider the cultural contexts of the children, as well as their own, so they can address biases in their practices. When educators have preconceived notions of how children will behave, they routinely misinterpret behavior in a negative way (Gilliam et al. 2016). That is especially true for children of color, and Black boys in particular. A pre-K program is a social environment with rules and norms regarding how we should behave. Some rules and norms are typical of the prevailing culture of early childhood education, and others are part of an educator's own philosophy and background. Children and families also come with their own rules and traditions. We often expect children to understand the expectations of conduct in early learning programs right away, but they don't know how to navigate and respond to our unwritten rules. Often, conflicts occur when a home culture and a school culture are not aligned.

Anti-bias Education and Anti-racism

An approach to handling diversity with wisdom is found in the concept of anti-bias education and in anti-racism efforts. With an anti-bias lens, educators explicitly work to end all forms of bias and discrimination. They do so not only through their own behaviors as adults but also by engaging children in constructing a fair and equitable world in their classrooms first (Derman-Sparks, Edwards, and Goins 2020). The anti-racism approach is about specifically identifying and addressing racial discrimination (Iruka et al. 2020). Here, too, adults must look at these big ideas through a developmentally appropriate perspective. That means addressing them at the level of a preschooler's cognitive and social capacity by reading books, telling stories, and facilitating real-life experiences of playing and learning in the classroom or family child care environment (Passe 2020).

Power to the Profession

The status of the early education workforce has come to greater attention since the pandemic, as educators' worth became obvious to working families who needed their services. NAEYC and its partners have been promoting a national collaboration with Power to the Profession and the Unifying Framework. The goal of this effort is to give the early childhood profession clarity and consistency around competencies and compensation (NAEYC 2020b). The workers in this field are not a monolith; they form a diverse group in terms of their educational backgrounds, philosophies, and cultures, yet they are united in their common mission to educate and care for the children who ultimately will end up in kindergarten.

We are on a positive path to pay attention to the cognitive and social skills of children, as well as their cultural and emotional well-being. We are also on a positive path to honor and support the educators themselves. We have been building on a strong foundation of research and compassionate spirit that will continue to improve. So, let's all get ready for kindergarten!

Introduction

Malika is standing in front of me, her brown eyes sparkling and her hands on her hips. "You know what? After I'm five, I am going to kindergarten!"

"You are? And what is that?" I ask.

"That's the big school, silly!" She rolls her eyes, incredulous at my ignorance of life's important things. "For the big kids, because I am big now."

Malika's mom sighs. "Yes, my baby is a big kid now." She looks proud and a little apprehensive at the same time. Her face tells me that going to kindergarten will be a big event for this family, even though Malika is going to the neighborhood elementary school, which is only five blocks from her home and where her brother is already in the second grade.

Going to kindergarten is the official beginning of a child's educational career, so it is an important part of child development and the family life cycle. It is also an important time for the school to make a good first impression. I want to start by presenting the beliefs that guide this book, which are based on current research, best practices, and my years of professional experience and observations:

The transition to kindergarten is not a one-time event.

A *transition* is a passage from one place or stage to another. It requires adapting feelings, thoughts, and behaviors from an old situation to a new one. When children enter kindergarten, they go from the intimate world of home or child care to the institutional world of education, especially if they attend a public school. Their families make the same adaptation. The transition is not a one-time event that happens on the first day of school; rather, the transition begins before children enter school and continues during their first year. The family, preschool program, and receiving elementary school all play important roles in making a smooth and productive transition. In order for this to happen, the three groups must know one another well, understand their different roles, share information, express their hopes, and work together for the children's benefit (Smythe-Leistico 2012).

Going to kindergarten is a developmental milestone.

Regardless of educational, cultural, or socioeconomic background, all families know about going to school, and all families want their children to do well in school. The entry to kindergarten is a milestone in the lives of families, likely the most important step since the child was born. Even for children who have attended a child care center or a family child care home, kindergarten is the beginning of their formal education. Starting kindergarten is exciting and scary at the same time. It can also be intimidating, particularly for families with lower levels of education and new immigrants who are not familiar with the culture and language of education.

All families want the best for their children.

Depending on their level of education and knowledge of the educational system, families have different ways of viewing kindergarten. Highly educated families tend to approach the entrance to kindergarten in the same way they would approach looking for a college. They conduct research and visit schools to choose the one that best meets their needs. Parents feel confident in their ability to advocate for their child, so they ask about the curriculum, visit the school's website to review its quality rating, and sign up to volunteer in the classroom.

Immigrant families, families in poverty, and families with low educational levels may be less familiar with the culture of education. These families may not be as aware of their choices, and they may not know how to conduct a search for a school. If their child already attends a preschool program, they rely on guidance from the staff. They also expect that the school system will help them and provide the best for their child. They are unsure about the rules and expectations schools have regarding family involvement.

Not all children have the same readiness for kindergarten.

Children have different experiences before they enter kindergarten. Those who participate in a quality preschool program (at a center or in family child care, public or private) are better prepared for school than those who attend a program of lesser quality. Children whose home environment is aligned with the expectations of kindergarten have easier transitions (NCPFCE 2013).

Early childhood programs have a big role in the transition to kindergarten.

A wide variety of programs including preschools, child care centers, family child care homes, Head Start, and early childhood programs in public schools all send children to kindergarten. Educators in these programs are usually familiar with the expectations of school readiness set by state or federal mandates, but they often feel disconnected from the expectations of the elementary schools in their community. They need to have as much information as possible about what happens in kindergarten classrooms. When there is a strong connection between the pre-K and the K–12 worlds, there are more opportunities to offer continuity for children and families (Ehrlich et al. 2021).

Schools must be ready for children and families.

Schools must have reasonable expectations of readiness, and they must be prepared to scaffold children's learning when they arrive at the door. Even though kindergarten is not part of compulsory education in every state, in 2021, about three-quarters of children in the United States attended a half-day or full-day public kindergarten (Institute of Education Sciences 2022). Just look at the big discount-store displays in August to realize the importance of schooling in our culture. Families view kindergarten as the official first year of school; yet not all schools treat children and families in the same way. Some schools are warm and welcoming places, while others are cold and unwelcoming. The latter is truer for immigrant families, families of color, and families in poverty. In focus groups, these families complain about a lack of respect and worry their children are not being accepted.

Family involvement is at its highest in kindergarten and tends to decline thereafter.

If they feel welcome and connected, families with kindergartners are open and ready to develop loyalty to the school and the school district. For the school district, this first year is the most critical opportunity to engage families as partners in education. The maxim that "you only have one chance to make a good first impression" applies here. Rather than only asking parents to adapt to the rules and views of the school, it is important for schools to learn what families want and expect. This honors parents' hopes and dreams for their children and engages them positively as partners in education right from the beginning (Doucet and Tudge 2007).

Coordination and planning make the transition to kindergarten easier.

Families expect a smooth path from preschool to kindergarten. Learning continuity is not only important for children, it is also the law for children in early childhood special education (Individuals with Disabilities

Education Act 2004) and for children of low-income families (Every Student Succeeds Act 2015). School districts and communities need a transition-to-kindergarten plan to help children and parents enter kindergarten. This plan needs to be based on current research and be simple enough for busy staff to implement.

A good transition to kindergarten benefits children, families, and schools.

Families with children who are in early childhood special education tend to receive the most comprehensive transition-to-kindergarten planning. Staff from both the preschool and the elementary school write and implement the individualized education program (IEP) with parents. This intense level of coordination may not be practical or necessary for all children; however, all children adapt faster and more easily when specific activities are designed to help them enter school. Parents who feel welcome and understand what is expected of them can support their children with more confidence. Teachers who get to know children and families well are more likely to have high expectations for student performance (Mancilla and Blanco 2022). Kindergarten is the entry to educational success.

All families sending their children to kindergarten have aspirations that their children will have a good education that prepares them for a good life. I have conducted many focus groups with parents who are most preoccupied with this question: will my child have a good job when they grow up? As the starting point to a school career, kindergarten is the first opportunity to pave the way for success in education and in life.

This Book Is for You

This book contains information about children's transition to kindergarten as well as practical ideas and activities for children and parents and for preschool, child care, and kindergarten staff. Based on your needs, you might use the entire book as a planning tool or use parts of it that are more relevant for your particular situation. The following list provides examples of how different people might apply what they read:

- Child care center directors or elementary school principals might find ideas for training staff on the transition to kindergarten.
- Family child care providers might use the vocabulary to explain school readiness to parents and find tips to give them on how to prepare their children for kindergarten.
- College instructors might include information in a syllabus to provide students with a comprehensive view of the transition to kindergarten.
- Parent educators might use the templates to prepare handouts for parent-child workshops.
- Preschool teachers might integrate the ideas into curricula for children preparing for kindergarten.
- Kindergarten teachers and preschool teachers might read the book together in a study group and develop a comprehensive transition-to-kindergarten plan.
- Community foundations that support a transition-to-kindergarten project might develop a one-day conference around the main topics covered in this book.
- Home visitors might find simple and fun activities to help child care providers and parents make the transition to kindergarten easier for their children.

Information and Practical Advice

When I present workshops to educators on the transition to kindergarten, I always begin by asking participants what they want to learn during their time with me. Their questions are usually very practical: What should we say to parents about school readiness? What are best practices for the transition to kindergarten? What are good ways to engage kindergarten teachers as partners? How do we help pre-K teachers better prepare children? How should we work with immigrant families who are new to our school system? What can the principal do to make the school more welcoming? What is school readiness?

Kindergarten used to be viewed as the rehearsal year for school, but it has become clear that kindergarten is a much more important time than once thought. As the early childhood field has evolved, professionals wonder if they're doing enough to prepare learners. My objective with *Ready for Kindergarten: A Tool Kit for Supporting Children and Families* is to give educators the tools they need to prepare learners.

How the Book Is Organized

Even though the book is organized in a sequence, you can consult the parts you find of most interest. Chapter 1 explores the concept of children being ready for school, as well as schools being ready for children and families. Chapter 2 examines kindergarten in the twenty-first century. Chapter 3 describes the characteristics of four-, five-, and six-year-old children, helping educators and caregivers understand their development, and it includes activities to facilitate the transition from preschool to kindergarten. Chapter 4 addresses the hopes and concerns parents have about kindergarten and includes activities for helping parents become active partners in their child's education. Chapter 5 covers the role of preschools and other sending programs in facilitating the transition to kindergarten. Chapter 6 offers strategic planning tools to help you prepare for the transition to kindergarten.

At the end of each chapter, discussion starters help you think more deeply about the information you've read and find practical solutions for your own challenges. You can use the questions individually or in discussions with colleagues. There are also checklists and handouts for you to use in your program or in training staff or families. I want this book to be of practical use to you, so feel free to modify the checklists and handouts for your own situation.

CHAPTER 1

Children Ready for School, Schools Ready for Children and Families

Omar is five years old. Today is his first day of school, and he is all dressed up for it. Last week, he went with his mom to a discount store to get his school uniform—khaki pants and a dark-blue polo shirt. The Head Start program he had attended since he was three years old gave him a Superman backpack as a graduation present. His grandparents bought him spiffy blue-and-white sneakers. His shiny black hair is neatly combed with a perfect part.

Is Omar ready for school? Is his school ready for him? School readiness goes both ways. Children need to be ready for school, *and* schools need to be ready for children and families.

When the words *school readiness* are mentioned, they often provoke tension, with a hint of exasperation. Everyone agrees with the concept, but the definition is not clearly articulated and also shifts. For example, at one point, children's ability to tie their shoes was high on the school readiness list, but with new shoe designs, that skill is no longer as much of a priority. Preschool educators, family child care providers, kindergarten teachers, administrators, and parents all want clarification.

The Concept of School Readiness for Children

As he gets off the bus, Omar looks shyly at the jolly principal greeting the children: "Welcome to school, children. I know it's going to be a good year for everyone!" Omar follows the line into the building and goes to room 102. Ms. Annie, the kindergarten teacher, says hello to him and shows him where to hang his backpack. She says, "I am so happy you are in my class, Omar. I remember you and your mom from the school picnic last week!" Omar grins. "I see you to picnic!" Then Ms. Annie takes him to the sign-in table. She believes in establishing routines on the first day. Omar chooses the blue marker, his favorite color, and confidently writes O-m-a-r. He used to do this every day at Head Start, and his mom helped him continue to practice during the summer.

When all the children have arrived, Ms. Annie brings them together for circle time to sing the good-morning song, which is sung in English to the tune of "Frère Jacques." At the end, Ms. Annie says, "That was 'good morning' in English! Now we are going to say 'good morning' in Spanish and Hmong, because some of you speak Spanish and Hmong at home too." Omar blurts out, "Buenos días!" Ms. Annie smiles and says, "Yes, let's all say 'Buenos días,' like Omar!"

Ms. Annie reads the book Look Out Kindergarten, Here I Come! *by Nancy Carlson, which is the same book Omar's Head Start teacher read last spring during the kindergarten theme. Omar listens with interest. He raises his hand when Ms. Annie asks the children if they feel the same as Henry, the main character, on this first day of school—a little bit scared and excited at the same time. At the end of the story, Ms. Annie shows the children the calendar. She leads them into counting to seven, since today is September 7. Omar counts along, concentrating on the numbers, moving his fingers. Is Omar ready for school?*

When I ask kindergarten teachers and principals what being ready for school means to them, they usually respond, "Just give me children who are well rested and fed, get along with others, take care of themselves, and know how to sit still, and I will teach them the academic skills they need." There is often a misalignment between the expectations of preschool and kindergarten educators regarding the importance of academic skills and social skills (Abry et al. 2015). At the same time, research shows that children who have poor language and literacy skills are at a big disadvantage when they enter school. For example, when children do not have a good vocabulary, they are not able to understand the books read to them (Tabors, Beals, and Weizman 2001). Further, if children are unable to understand the story, there may be little to hold their attention. If this is the cause of their inability to sit still at circle time, attempts at teaching them to be quiet and to sit "crisscross applesauce" may not necessarily improve their behavior.

The School Readiness Road

The best approach to thinking about school readiness is to look at children in a holistic way (Friedman et al. 2021). The *whole child* includes body, mind, and emotions. In educational terms, it means addressing physical, cognitive, and social-emotional development. We need to nurture development so children learn specific skills and behaviors with the understanding that they will be on the road to school readiness. To help teachers and providers assess children's abilities, there are various comprehensive child observation checklists, such as the Work Sampling System, Teaching Strategies' GOLD, or the Child Observation Record (COR), each of which has a reliable system for indicating overall child development.

The developmental perspective asserts that children will not achieve the same degree of school readiness at the exact same time, nor will they move at the same pace. Still, we know typically developing children will have the same skills and behaviors around the same chronological age (Minnesota Department of Education 2017).

I like to think about school readiness as being like a cross-country race where there is no mad sprinting but a steady, intentional pace. This analogy comes to mind because my daughter is an amateur long-distance runner, and my husband and I have watched her race many times. Picture the runners at the starting point. They have different body types, running styles, clothes, shoes, and warm-up techniques. They probably have had different training programs, diets, and advice from coaches. But there they all are, on a cloudy Sunday morning, at point A on the road to point Z, with several water stations for rest and rehydration along the way.

Watching the race, driving from station to station, we recognize many of the runners. We notice they have different levels of support. Some have coaches who run alongside. Others have relatives and friends on the side of the road who encourage them by calling their names. Others do not have direct supporters, but strangers, like me, who shout general praise: "Keep going. You are almost there. Good running, number 342!" Even though the racers are running at different speeds and with various forms, one rule is clear: all participants are going in the same direction toward the same point. A few reach the finish line well before those in the large pack, who arrive within a compact time frame, and a few pull in at the end. All the participants are proud to have finished, having accomplished so much!

Doing well in school is necessary for success in life. Early educators can help children achieve success in a thoughtful way, like the coaches who run alongside the runners. The job of educators is to use developmentally appropriate practices to teach. In other words, educators need to offer activities that are meaningful, fun, and physically and mentally possible for the children to do. Educators also need to scaffold, or gently guide, children to the next step of learning—not too hard, not too easy, but just right. Good education should not be one-size-fits-all, with only one teaching approach for all children, regardless of whether they are learning. And it is important to avoid extremes. Good education should not be completely individualized, either, waiting for children to learn on their own time. Thoughtful teachers scaffold children's learning by offering manageable challenges. It is unreasonable to show four-year-olds how to write their names once and expect them to do it on their own. It is also unreasonable to let them scribble randomly rather than give them repeated opportunities to practice forming the letters of their names and be successful in spelling their names.

The Role of Language and Literacy in School Readiness

The classic National Research Council report *Preventing Reading Difficulties in Young Children* helped shape the definition of school readiness we still hold today by highlighting the importance of language and early literacy in learning to read (Snow, Burns, and Griffin 1998). It makes it clear that the foundation for academic skills rests on the abilities to talk, read, and write. For example, in order to write a story about butterflies, the child has to ask questions about butterflies (talk), do research in books or on the internet (read), and put ideas on paper or on the computer (write).

The best tool for getting along with others and managing our own behavior is language. Sara, who is four years old, says (talk) she wants to play with the truck that Peter is holding. She notices he is not letting it go on his own. She has to make a choice: she can grab the truck from Peter (not talk), play with something else (not talk), or say, "Peter, I want a turn with the truck" (talk). When we tell children to use their words, it is always as the alternative to the more primitive behaviors of hitting, grabbing, or whining. Without effective language and communication skills, it is impossible to achieve good social-emotional development. That is why there is a special emphasis on language as the key to school readiness.

Early Learning Standards and Indicators of Progress

Enough research-based information exists to give educators a good idea of what children should know. From this research, thoughtful early childhood educators have developed national and international early learning standards and indicators of progress. For example, the Minnesota Department of Education's *Early Childhood Indicators of Progress* (2017) gives a comprehensive overview of what children from birth to kindergarten need to know. The standards describe expectations of children in six domains: Social and Emotional Development; Approaches to Learning; Language, Literacy, and Communications; Creativity and the Arts; Cognitive Development: Mathematics, Science, and Social Systems; and Physical and Movement Development. These domains complement one another and are critical for overall development. Since children grow at individual rates but in a predictable way, most children will meet the majority of expectations for developmental standards by the time they enter kindergarten. As of 2022, three-quarters of states had established standards of learning for early childhood, some focusing mostly on language and literacy. The emphasis on language is important, as many of the indicators can be mastered only with the help of good language skills.

Find out about your own state's development of early learning standards. The Center on Enhancing Early Learning Outcomes (CEELO) has a comprehensive website (http://ceelo.org/state-map) that allows you to search by state or territory and find out about early learning standards in your area. Alternatively, go directly to the website of the Department of Education of your state.

I want to share some items as examples of the preschool developmental milestones from Minnesota's *Early Childhood Indicators of Progress* (Minnesota Department of Education 2017). The understanding behind the standards is that children are on a continuum developmentally. The language of the standards, describing children's skills and behaviors, can seem abstract and technical, so I have added vignettes to illustrate how these apply to what children are doing in real life. To provide more context as you read, think of a four-year-old child you know well and imagine his or her actions.

https://edocs.dhs
.state.mn.us/lfserver
/Public/DHS-7596A
-ENG

Social and Emotional Development

The Social and Emotional Development domain includes the components Self and Emotional Awareness; Self-Management; and Social Understanding and Relationships. The indicators for pre-schoolers focus on how children show confidence and self-direction; how they identify gender and self as part of a family, community, and culture; their ability to make choices; their verbal expression of needs and emotions; their responses to changing behavioral expectations; and how they are beginning to manage conflicts in social interactions.

Self and Emotional Awareness

> *Joey is on the jungle gym. He crosses over the narrow bridge. He advances slowly and carefully, one step at a time, balancing with his arms. When he gets to the other side, he smiles proudly, throws up his arms, and shouts, "Look, I did it!"*

Self-Management

> *Lisa has been working for ten minutes on a complicated puzzle. After several tries, she cannot complete it. She goes to the teacher, puts her hands on her hips, and says with a scowl, "Ms. Barbara, I am really, really, really frustrated! I can't do it. Help me, please!"*

Social Understanding and Relationships

> *Paula observes quietly as two children—a girl and a boy—make vegetable soup in the housekeeping area. After a few minutes, Paula approaches them and asks, "Can I play?" The children ignore her. She stands, smiles, gets a little closer, and says softly*

but assertively, "I make chicken soup." The boy notices, looks at her, and responds, "Okay." Paula joins the little group, and they all continue to play together.

Approaches to Learning

The Approaches to Learning domain includes the components Initiative and Curiosity; Attentiveness, Engagement, and Persistence; Creativity; and Processing and Utilizing Information. For preschoolers, the indicators focus on how children show their eagerness to investigate new things, engage in play with peers for extended periods of time, persist, experiment with new ways to combine materials, and contribute relevant information to discussions.

Creativity

Daniela's first language is Spanish, and Poua's first language is Hmong, and they both are learning English. They are playing in the beauty shop, pretending to put on nail polish, when Daniela says, "Red." However, the small bottle they are using is white. Poua looks around knowingly, goes to the art shelf, brings back a red marker, and hands it to Daniela, saying, "Red." They scribble on the bottle until it is red, giggling. Then they happily apply the imaginary "red" nail polish they have created together.

Language, Literacy, and Communications

The Language, Literacy, and Communications domain includes the components Listening and Understanding (Receptive Language); Communicating and Speaking (Expressive Language); Emergent Reading; and Writing. Preschoolers' vocabulary is fast expanding and their conversation skills are improving. They can express their needs and wants in clear language with accurate grammar and syntax. Preschoolers enjoy being read to and telling their own stories. They also begin to make sense of letters and sounds and discover wordplay and writing beyond scribbling.

Communicating and Speaking

> *During free-play time, Raoul and Matteo are making plans for a weekend visit to Matteo's house. They discuss what toys Raoul should bring to "play mechanics in the auto shop." Then the teacher calls the boys for story time and reads a book about polar bears, a completely different topic from their previous conversation. They listen attentively, make comments, and ask questions about polar bears.*

Emergent Reading

> *During circle time, Sally sits in the teacher's chair and begins to "read" a book to three other children, who listen to her intently. She points to the pictures and follows the text with a plastic pointer, describing each page from memory. When Sally reaches the end of the story, she proclaims, "The end!"*

Writing

> *Rosa and Maia are in the dramatic play area, which is set up as a pizza parlor. One is a cook, and the other is a waitress. They call out to Maggie, the classroom aide, "Do you want to order pizza?" As soon as Maggie sits down, Maia hands her the menu and explains the different types of pizza, pointing at the pictures. She scribbles the order on her notepad and takes it to Rosa, who studies it carefully and asks, "Is this order for one or two people? I only see one here." When Maia confirms the order is for two customers, Rosa adds her own note on the paper and goes to the kitchen to prepare the pizzas.*

The Arts

The Arts domain includes the components Exploring the Arts; Using the Arts to Express Ideas and Emotions; and Self-Expression in the Arts. The indicators for preschoolers focus on how children intentionally use the arts, develop the vocabulary to describe their own creations, and begin to combine artistic elements.

Exploring the Arts

> *Marysol has been painting at the easel for ten minutes. This spring in this classroom, children have been studying nature, including landscape illustrations. The teacher says, "Marysol, tell me about your painting." Marysol responds, "This is the yellow sun and a tree and flowers, and the sun makes the flowers grow."*

Cognitive Development: Mathematics

The Mathematics portion of the Cognitive Development domain includes the components Number Knowledge; Measurement; Patterns; Geometry and Spatial Thinking; and Data Analysis. The indicators for preschoolers focus on their increasing language capabilities and use of mathematical terms to describe and make sense of their world. They recite numbers and count objects. They identify geometric shapes and use the language of measurement. They develop sorting strategies and create patterns using various rules and skills. Mathematics is highly correlated to the Language, Literacy, and Communications domain.

Number Knowledge

> *Pao and Arthur are standing at the whiteboard. Pao is counting aloud, "One, two, three, five." Arthur scribbles symbols with a marker to represent numbers. Suddenly, they realize their counting is not sequential. They go back to the manipulatives table and practice counting small teddy bears very slowly: "One, two, three,*

four, five—we forgot four. We forgot four!" The children laugh, sat-isfied with their discovery, and go back to the whiteboard to write the number four between the three and the five.

Data Analysis

Jill is at the water table, where the teacher has set up floating and sinking objects. Jill tries to sink the small red boat with her hands, but it keeps floating back up when she lets go. After a few tries, she decides to put a big stone on the boat. The boat goes to the bottom. Jill looks surprised and then lifts the stone and watches the boat come back up. She keeps experimenting with different-sized stones. When another child joins her, Jill comments, "The big stone makes the boat sink. It can float with the little stone."

Cognitive Development: Social Systems

The Social Systems portion of the Cognitive Development domain includes the components Community, People, and Relationships; Change over Time; Environment; Economics; and Technology. The indicators for preschoolers focus on their developing understanding of their identities and of belonging in different groups, how they are learn-ing to follow rules and routines, how they are showing interest in family culture, and how they are participating in turn-taking and negotiation.

Community, People, and Relationships

Luisito is Latino. Mohamed and Ali are Somali. They all live in a rural community in the Midwest. At lunchtime, Mohamed and Ali announce they want to speak Spanish like Luisito. They make up words to end with "-to" and "-ta." All three giggle as they con-tinue to experiment with the sounds of Spanish. When the teacher points out that people speak different languages in different parts of the world, Luisito confirms, "My grandma speaks Spanish in Mexico."

Physical and Movement Development

The Physical and Movement Development domain includes Gross Motor and Fine Motor components. The indicators for preschoolers focus on how children show their increasing coordination and balance as they walk, run, climb, hop, jump, and gallop and as they kick, throw, catch, and bounce balls. They show their increasing ability to use hands and fingers to manipulate puzzle pieces, draw and write, and put on articles of clothing. They also become aware of the importance of health and well-being.

Gross Motor and Fine Motor

> *Under the cool arcade of a California preschool, Tomi is riding a tricycle, controlling the speed with his strong little legs and expertly avoiding obstacles. He stops at the play farmers market set up by his teacher. He buys zucchini and red peppers. "Vegetables are good. They help you grow strong," Tomi says. Then he pays for the vegetables by writing his name on a check.*

An Analysis of Omar's School Readiness

Think about Omar again and his first day of kindergarten. I have prepared a summary to help analyze his school readiness using the *Early Childhood Indicators of Progress* (Minnesota Department of Education 2017), including concrete examples to assess his experiences and to imagine how school readiness would look in very practical terms.

Early Learning Standard	Summary of Critical Early Childhood Indicators of Progress	What We See Omar Doing
Social and Emotional Development	Interacts easily with other children and adults Uses words to resolve conflicts Participates successfully as a group member	Smiles Responds to teacher Greets classmates by waving Sits in circle
Approaches to Learning	Is curious Takes risks Approaches tasks with flexibility, imagination, and inventiveness Is persistent and reflective	Chooses a marker in his favorite color to show how he writes his name
Language, Literacy, and Communications	Uses language to communicate needs Interacts socially with others Shares ideas, thoughts, and feelings Builds on spoken and written language abilities	Responds nonverbally to the principal Speaks to the teacher in telegraphic English Says good morning in his home language, Spanish Writes his name Remembers the story
The Arts	Uses various media and materials for exploration and creative expression Creates Responds Evaluates	Shows a marked preference for the color blue Chooses the marker he likes best
Cognitive Development (Mathematics, Social Systems, and Scientific Thinking)	Acquires information Thinks logically Orders and puts in sequence Understands measurement Engages in scientific thinking and problem solving Understands social systems	Understands counting as a concept Knows that not all his classmates speak Spanish
Physical and Movement Development	Develops large-muscle control Hones small-muscle control Is in good physical health	Uses small muscles to hold the marker and write his name Forms letters correctly Passes the preschool health screening Has all the required immunizations

Even though this is only Omar's first day of kindergarten and therefore we have not observed all his abilities, we can start to picture where he is on the road to being ready for school. Many of his behaviors are due to his maturity as a five-year-old. Some behaviors are because of work his preschool teachers and family have done up to this point. And other behaviors can be accredited to positive connections that his elementary school's staff made with him and his family.

While following his own developmental path, Omar has had many opportunities for learning. The results of this are the developmentally appropriate social and academic skills he demonstrates. Socially, he seems comfortable with new adults like the principal and teacher, he can follow directions, and he functions well in a group of peers. Academically, he can write his name, he knows how to count to five, and he understands the story.

Omar has the skills to enter kindergarten. How the preschool program and his mother have prepared him is one side of the story. In order to succeed in the rest of his educational career, he will need the strong support of his elementary school.

Play and Learning Standards

While the focus on learning standards is good, beware of wanting to apply standards in a narrow way. In a backlash to laissez-faire free play, in which children interact very little with teachers and there is not much instruction, some preschool educators are choosing worksheets and flash card games at the expense of play (Miller and Almon 2009). Teachers rationalize that they are responding to the mandate to focus on the basics, but this is a faulty rationale since educational and psychological research shows that in order to get smart, young children need to touch, feel, hear, and talk. We want to see children learn the basics—talking, reading, and writing—*while* they play. Children need time, space, activities, and adult guidance to learn through meaningful, hands-on experiences. When our son, a chemical engineer, was attending college, part of the curriculum included playing with Lego bricks, the purpose of which was to spark creativity and problem-solving skills. All the more reason to expect preschoolers and kindergartners to play with Lego bricks too!

As early childhood teachers and providers, we will have successfully done our jobs—preparing children for school—only when we've remained vigilant about the quality of play in our preschool programs, child care homes, and centers (Campbell et al. 2018).

Equity in Learning for Children in the Twenty-First Century

The first recommendation of the 2020 NAEYC position statement *Developmentally Appropriate Practice* is to create a caring, equitable community of learners by being sensitive to the individual development and learning needs of all children.

School data and research show that many children who are experiencing poverty, children of color, and children of immigrants do not do well in school. They are not ready for school before they enter, and once there, they have increasing difficulties academically and socially (Brooks-Gunn 2008). They are not proficient at grade level in math and reading, and they are more likely to be suspended for inappropriate behavior.

Kindergarten teachers describe these children as having more difficulties in adjusting to school than children not experiencing barriers. This situation requires an intentional planning effort to ensure all children are well taught in a system that is struggling to meet their needs. Not only do educators need to pay attention to the developmental needs of children, but they also have to be competent at addressing, valuing, and using cultural and linguistic differences to teach. They must use an

www.redleafpress
.org/Creating
-Diversity-Rich
-Environments
-for-Young
-Children-P2301
.aspx

equity and diversity lens in their curriculum so children have opportunities to see themselves in it (NAEYC 2020a; Passe 2020). Detailed explanations and strategies for doing so are described in my book *Creating Diversity-Rich Environments for Young Children.*

The Concept of Ready Schools

Last winter, Ms. Annie, Omar's kindergarten teacher, attended a joint-staff workshop with the principal of the school where she teaches and with Head Start staff. The idea originated at a school district principals' meeting earlier in the fall. The workshop topic and agenda were straightforward—share expectations and classroom routines. After a general introduction and information about the demographics of their community, the teachers, paraprofessionals, and administrators divided into small groups to discuss what they teach as well as how they teach in their programs and classrooms. They also talked about how they work with families.

The education professionals reviewed a checklist as a guide to define the activities that helped children and families transition from pre-K to kindergarten. At the end of two hours, the evaluations showed the participants felt productive and were grateful to know each other's approach better. A recommendation was made to have a similar workshop every year and invite more preschool programs from the area.

In 1998, the National Education Goals Panel recommended "Ten Keys to Ready Schools" in its report *Ready Schools* (Shore 1998, 5). Today these recommendations are still relevant and include the following:

1. "Ready schools smooth the transition between home and school.
2. Ready schools strive for continuity between early care and education programs and elementary schools.

3. Ready schools help children learn and make sense of their complex and exciting world.

4. Ready schools are committed to the success of every child.

5. Ready schools are committed to the success of every teacher and every adult who interacts with children during the school day.

6. Ready schools introduce or expand approaches that have been shown to raise achievement.

7. Ready schools are learning organizations that alter practices and programs if they do not benefit children.

8. Ready schools serve children in communities.

9. Ready schools take responsibility for results.

10. Ready schools have strong leadership."

So, is Omar's school ready for him? Using this list, let's see in what ways Omar's new school is ready for children:

- The principals in the school district made a plan to address continuity in their community between the preschool and the elementary school worlds. The principals convened staff from preschools and elementary schools to meet each other and share their work so they could be more successful (#2, #5, #8, and #10).

- Ms. Annie and the principal participated in joint training with the Head Start staff to coordinate the curriculum (#2).

- The school organized a picnic before the first day so children and their families could meet the staff and visit the school (#1 and #4).

- Ms. Annie did the sign-in activity and read a book, following the preschool routine in the Head Start classroom (#1).

- Ms. Annie acknowledged and welcomed the cultural and linguistic diversity in her classroom (#3).

With the information from this first day, we can see that seven out of ten items have been addressed. Omar's school is intentional in getting ready for children and their families, which is not a simple task.

Ready Schools Need Ready Personnel

Schools are more than buildings. Schools are places where teachers, educational assistants, nurses, custodians, social workers, cooks, secretaries, bus drivers, and principals work directly with children and families. These staff members are important in students' lives. They interact with children every day in classrooms, in hallways, in lunchrooms, and on the bus. Staff members have the power to either give discouraging messages or provide encouraging support. In order to be ready for children who are entering kindergarten and their families, school personnel have to prepare themselves first. There is a lot they think about: Who are the children coming to our school? What do they need? Where were they before they came to us? How will our teaching methods work for them? Who are their families? What are their expectations? What do we expect from children and families? How do we communicate? The most important question, which is not always asked explicitly, is whether we think these children can really learn and succeed.

Kindergarten teachers tend to rate children of color lower in social competence (Vitiello et al. 2022). This happens when children respond inaccurately to the communication style of the school culture. For example, children may be used to a direct style at home, such as, "Ramon, put away your toys now." But often teachers use an indirect style, by asking questions, such as, "Ramon, would you like to put away the toys?" If Ramon wants to continue to play and truthfully answers, "No," he will likely be labeled as defiant.

In diverse countries, such as the United States, demographic patterns are not static. Children, families, and staff from many cultures mix and interact in schools. This creates challenges for educational systems that are mandated to teach *all* children.

Education Is a Complex Professional Field

The field of education for noneducators is as complex as any other professional field, including medicine or law. School websites, brochures, and staff use jargon such as *interdisciplinary, curriculum objectives, math recovery,* and *robotics electives.* Jargon is a tool of the "culture of power." Families also want to know what these words mean and how they will help children learn. For that, schools have to include them intentionally.

Being part of the culture of power means knowing the rules that define talking, writing, and interacting—all of which are important to getting things done and being part of the inner circle (Delpit 1995). This is in contrast to how families feel when they are not as familiar with the culture of education.

To borrow a phrase from *Other People's Children: Cultural Conflict in the Classroom* (Delpit 1995), many teachers are teaching other people's children. This idea refers not only to racial and cultural differences but also to being distanced from children by education and social class. I believe it is important to be aware of the issue so it can be addressed directly and appropriately in preservice training and in continuing professional development. Schools can then be fully ready to welcome all children and families.

Families' Hopes and Anxieties

When children enter kindergarten, their families want to know what the rules are so they can help their children achieve, because all families want their children to do well in school. When I conduct workshops and focus groups, I see that parents, regardless of background, have similar anxieties. Families look to educators to serve as their guides through the culture of education:

- "We cannot judge the quality of education. We are not experts, and we just hope that the school provides quality education."
- "I want to help my son be a better student, but I don't know how. You need to tell us how to do that."
- "I don't want the teacher to love my child—I already love her. I want the teacher to *teach* my daughter what she needs to learn."

Family-School Partnerships Are a Special Effort

The barriers to developing good family-school partnerships fall into two categories: structure and attitude (Christenson 1999). On the structural side, the school staff may not have had training in how to work with parents. Also, schools may not provide an activities schedule that is convenient for parents. As a result, the opportunities to partner are few. The communication system that tells families what is happening at school may be written and formal, using newsletters and flyers (paper or digital); whereas parents might use an informal word-of-mouth system in person and on the phone. In one focus group, a Somali father said that his community is so well connected by cell phone that if his son's school wanted to let him know of an important event, they could call his cousin in Kenya and within minutes he, the father, would hear about it in Minnesota!

Sometimes the economic, educational, and social distance between families and teachers causes misunderstandings. For example, I once heard kindergarten teachers lament that Latino families send their little girls dressed up in frilly dresses and patent leather shoes on the first day of school. They commented that these parents just don't value education and don't understand that in kindergarten children do messy activities, which is how they learn. These teachers needed to hear the reasons why Latina girls come dressed up on the first day of school. They needed to know that the parents wanted to present their little girls in the best light to make a good impression on the teacher. The children were dressed up and had their hair combed in fancy ways to look beautiful and attractive. The parents also assume that at the "big" school their children sit neatly at their desks to learn. These parents show they value education when they send their children to school well kept and well behaved—these are the qualities they believe make children ready for school. The problem is not that the parents don't value education, but that they don't know how young children learn and how kindergarten teachers teach. They don't have the inside information.

Educators as Cultural Guides

A big part of Omar's positive experience with the transition to kindergarten was the guidance his mother, Olga, also received. While Omar was in the preschool program at Head Start, Olga was personally invited to monthly events from January to April. Each month, one topic was offered on a schedule that included morning, afternoon, and evening options. These options made it convenient for her to attend the workshops, since her job as a grocery-store cashier changed shifts every ten days.

In addition to information on child development, Olga learned about how to choose a school and received tips for helping children transition to kindergarten. She liked best the session where a kindergarten teacher and a principal came to talk about how schools work. Olga learned about the differences between Head Start and elementary school and about the expectations for parent involvement. She understood that in the school, parents have to take more initiative in connecting with staff than they did in Head Start. In general, schools do not have as many family liaisons to help parents. The highlight was a PowerPoint slide showing the road from kindergarten to college, as well as the advice of the principal, who said, "If you do all the things we have talked about, your child will have the best chance of going to college."

Throughout the winter, spring, and summer, Olga received valuable advice and new ideas to help her understand the culture of education. Both the preschool and elementary staff acted as cultural guides to an aspect of life with which she had little experience. They did so in a direct way, knowing she had high aspirations for her child's education but little knowledge on how to navigate the educational system.

Omar's mom felt encouraged and motivated to attend the orientation at the school, play with Omar on the school playground during the summer, help Omar write his name at home, and take him to the library story times. All of these activities made sense to her in the context of helping Omar over the long term with his education.

Discussion Starters

- Pretend that you are taking a trip to the Grand Canyon and you are hiring a guide. What do you want from this guide? What do you want the guide to say and do? What characteristics do you expect the guide to have? Make a list. How would the items listed apply to educators helping parents learn about the educational system?
- Find and read the early learning standards for your state. Reflect on how your knowledge of the early learning standards presently guides the way you work with children.
- If this is the first time you are reviewing such standards, how will they guide your work in the future? Choose three indicators you want to focus on.

CHAPTER 2

Kindergarten in the Twenty-First Century

At a Kindergarten Association conference, I am presenting a transition-to-kindergarten workshop to early childhood educators and kindergarten teachers. A show of hands reveals that the participants are between twenty-five and sixty years old, and the majority have more than ten years of working experience. As a warm-up activity, I ask participants to share their kindergarten memories with the person sitting next to them. After a moment of silent reflection, a crescendo of voices fills the room. Faces are animated—some smiling, others frowning. There is laughter and empathetic listening. Everyone is engaged, and I hate to break up the conversation, but we need to move on.

To the larger group, participants present the main points of their exchanges. First, they all remembered kindergarten! For many, it was a sweet time of playing, making friends, and sharing snacks in the care of a friendly teacher. For a few, kindergarten was a painful time, saying goodbye to their families, or not having nice teachers. Only two people in the group did not go to kindergarten at all; their families kept them at home until first grade.

A Brief History of Kindergarten

Friedrich Froebel, a German educator, opened the first kindergarten in Blankenburg, Germany, in 1837. During the 1830s and 1840s, he developed his vision for kindergarten based on the ideas of French philosopher Jean-Jacques Rousseau and Swiss educator Johann Heinrich Pestalozzi. These progressive education reformers introduced the concept that children were naturally good and active learners. At the time, this thinking was quite radical. The common belief until then had been that children were little creatures who needed stern handling to become good adults. Play was seen as a waste of time and proof that children should be tamed so they could be more productive.

Undaunted, Froebel argued that teachers should use music, nature studies, stories, and dramatic play to teach children. He encouraged the use of crafts and manipulatives, such as small building blocks and puzzles. He also promoted the idea of circle time for children to learn in a group. Froebel proposed that children acquire cognitive and social skills by using their natural curiosity and desire to learn. He believed women had the best sensitivity and qualities to work with young children in developing their emotional skills. Consequently, Froebel opened a training school just for women.

Froebel's ideas were so new that the government closed all kindergartens in 1851, fearing a socialist revolutionary movement. Nevertheless, the concept spread quickly throughout the rest of the world, and by the end of the nineteenth century, many countries had started kindergartens for middle-class children. Then, between 1900 and the start of World War I, England and France began to establish free kindergartens for poor children. Kindergartens also reopened in Germany at the end of the nineteenth century, where they still serve children who are three to six years old. The word *kindergarten* means "garden of children," a beautiful metaphor for what happens there—children growing like flowers and plants, nurtured by a positive environment with good soil, rain, and sun, as well as an attentive gardener.

In the United States, Margarethe Schurz opened the first kindergarten in Watertown, Wisconsin, in 1856 for her immigrant German community. This kindergarten caught the attention of Elizabeth Peabody, who started the first American English-language kindergarten in Boston in 1860. Then, in large cities, charities began to fund private kindergartens to care for the three- to six-year-old children of immigrant factory workers, which meant these children were healthy, clean, fed, and clothed. The goal was not so much to teach reading and writing as to develop overall cognitive and social-emotional skills—the beginning of considering the *whole child*.

Saint Louis, Missouri, was the first city to have a public kindergarten in 1873. By 1914, the beginning of World War I, all the major American urban school systems had publicly funded kindergartens that were open for five-year-olds. Mississippi was the last state to offer public kindergarten, in 1986. Today, kindergarten is available in all states. Forty-two states mandate that every school district must offer it. Children are eligible to attend kindergarten at the age of five, although some states allow for four-year-olds. In many states, the compulsory age for starting school ranges between six and eight years old, so families can decide to skip kindergarten and enter school in the first or second grade. In 2021, about four million children were enrolled in half-day or full-day kindergarten in the United States.

The Philosophical Foundation for the American Kindergarten

Many educators and psychologists have influenced the philosophy of the modern American kindergarten, including John Dewey, Maria Montessori, Erik Erikson, Jean Piaget, and Lev Vygotsky. To summarize and combine their ideas and create the ideal pre-K and kindergarten program, this is what the composite list would look like:

Theorist	*Teaching and Learning Practices*
Dewey (1859–1952)	• Teachers share their knowledge with children. • Children learn by building on their knowledge of the world, adding new information by exploring actively.
Montessori (1870–1952)	• Teachers provide child-centered environments, with materials, books, and toys that are accessible, orderly, and beautiful. • Children learn by structuring their own time, being responsible for their environment, and using repetition.
Erikson (1902–1994)	• Teachers set clear expectations, encourage children to be independent, and give feedback on learning. • Children develop purpose and competence by using real tools and solving real problems.
Piaget (1896–1980)	• Teachers provide open-ended activities and questions to help children learn to think. • Children move their thinking from perception to reasoning.
Vygotsky (1896–1934)	• Teachers provide positive challenges and support (scaffolding) to stretch learning. • Children learn through interaction, experimentation, and conversation.

Common Points of Quality for Pre-K and Kindergarten

- Curriculum is meaningful and relevant to children.
- Activity is purposeful.
- Learning can be uncomfortable.
- Learning becomes fun when children are engaged and supported.
- There is a balance of child-initiated and teacher-led activities.
- Children learn through real-life exploration and problem solving.
- Free play is not free; it is active learning during an extended period of time where children choose among equally valuable activities.
- Children are challenged in a positive way.
- Play is a child's work.
- Language is essential to learning.
- Interactions with adults and peers are important for learning.
- Learning and growing does not happen naturally; it needs to be planned and nurtured.

Table content drawn from Mooney, Carol Garhart. 2013. *Theories of Childhood: An Introduction to Dewey, Montessori, Erikson, Piaget, and Vygotsky*, Second Edition. St. Paul, MN: Redleaf Press.

The Reality of Current Kindergartens

You may be wondering why the transition from preschool to kindergarten is a big deal if both preschool and kindergarten fall under the category of early childhood education. By definition, shouldn't they already be aligned? This is not always the case. The legacy of these thinkers—Dewey, Montessori, Erikson, Piaget, and Vygotsky—is visible in many kindergartens, although there are some misinterpretations along the way (Mooney 2013).

Some classrooms are perfect examples of the previous table's right column, "Common Points of Quality for Pre-K and Kindergarten"; however, the quality of classrooms is vastly variable. Some classrooms have a strong thematic curriculum with well-integrated activities and a sensitive, intentional teacher. Children learn best in this situation. Other classrooms have a curriculum that is an eclectic collection of unrelated activities presented by a warm and friendly teacher. The children may not be learning much, but the emphasis is on fun. Still other classrooms have a curriculum that is not relevant to the children and is presented by a teacher who is unaware of children's learning needs or inattentive to them. This lack of consistency does not serve children well.

New Academic Pressures

Kindergarten is under pressure as the door to the "serious learning years." Should we keep the more relaxed pace of pre-K, or should we "push down" the first-grade curriculum, applying it to kindergarten in an effort to speed up learning? Some people worry that we may be pressuring children too much, while other people wonder if children will ever catch up if they are not yet ready for kindergarten.

As the movement for accountability in education grows, many states have aligned learning expectations for kindergarten with elementary and secondary standards. At first glance, learning standards in kindergarten do not appear to be that different from the early learning standards listed in chapter 1.

Nostalgically, adults may perceive kindergarten as the basis for formal education. Most people remember it as a time to make friends and learn the rules of school before the "real work" begins. Kindergarten teachers now are feeling increasing pressure to prepare children for first grade, with prescribed math and reading curricula and an intense schedule of assessments. Kindergarten is the bridge between early education and elementary education; it is not a practice grade anymore. It is serious business.

Full-Day versus Half-Day Kindergarten

As of this writing, more states have expanded kindergarten to a full day. And in 2021, a bill was introduced in Congress for funding universal full-day kindergarten in the United States. However, kindergarten availability depends on state and local choices, as well as families' choices in some cases. Kindergarten was conceived as a half-day program, based on the idea that a full day of school was too long for young children. A half day was supposed to ensure a low-key introduction to school, with longer days starting in first grade. The argument that children cannot handle full-time schedules outside of their home is not as relevant anymore. As families' work patterns have changed, more children are now in full-day child care and are accustomed to a full-day schedule. Many school districts have added universal pre-K classrooms.

Kindergarten as the Bridge between Preschool and Elementary School

Children's experiences vary greatly before they enter kindergarten. They may be at home with mom or dad or at grandma's house. They may be in a large child care center or in a small family child care home. They may attend Head Start or a public school readiness program. Or they may even be in a combination of places, depending on their families' income, mobility, and needs for child care.

Preschool quality is unreliable in our decentralized system (NIEER 2021). Some centers and homes have teachers and providers who are caring and sensitive. They scaffold children's learning with meaningful activities and language, using a research-based curriculum in a literacy-rich environment with lots of play. They assess children's learning with developmentally appropriate tools. In other settings, children may spend hours on end watching television in a barren environment with a caregiver who does not speak or read to them. Or they may be required to spend time at tables doing worksheets that they don't understand. At the same time, big efforts have been made with the QRIS movement. Many states have established a star rating system (usually ranging from one to four) that informs families about the quality of the child care center or family child care home. That is good news as programs are held to higher expectations of quality with each star (Jenkins et al. 2021). While slow, the momentum is positive.

The Impact of Home on School Preparation

Children's home lives prepare them for school in different ways too. Some children have literacy- and language-rich homes with many books. They have parents and relatives who talk, read, and write with them in ways similar to how learning happens at school. These children learn the basics of conversation, critical thinking, and making choices from the time they are babies. They receive encouragement for being learners and thinkers. Their parents tend to have high levels of education and are literate in English and in their home languages. In these families, children usually practice school-like activities such as reading, drawing, scribbling, and playing board games or language-based what-if games. The following interaction between a dad and his preschool son illustrates the point:

Son: What are we doing, Daddy?

Father: We are waiting for the elevator. It will take us to the third floor. That's where we parked the car.

Son: Where are we now?

Father: We are on the first floor. Do you see the numbers next to the door? One, two, three, four, five. We are going to three. It's here. Let's get in.

Father: (*in the elevator*) Do you see the numbers again? Can you push the "three" button?

Son: (*squealing in delight*) I did it, Daddy! I pushed the three!

Father: Yeah! Three, like you. You are three too! You are actually three and a half—that's more than three.

Son: (*following the numbers as the elevator ascends*) Look, we are at three.

Father: Yes, we are here. Let's go quickly . . .

We can safely say this child is getting ready for kindergarten. His father is teaching him numbers and having conversations in a natural way. Not every child has opportunities like this, and it becomes necessary for early educators to ensure such opportunities are provided in early childhood classrooms or homes.

Many children are well cared for in nurturing homes but yet are not engaged in preliteracy activities in the normal course of their day. Here's an example of a Hmong father's concerns about his children. The father's grandparents care for his children while he and his wife work during the day. He said, "My grandparents are nice people. They are good about feeding the children and making sure they are safe, but the children watch television all day. I am not sure that's good for them."

Some children arrive at the kindergarten door with the language and social skills necessary to learn, and others are behind. In many kindergarten classrooms, teachers may see levels of language and literacy development between that of a three-year-old and an eight-year-old (Neuman, Copple, and Bredekamp 1999). As the bridge between the pre-K and the K–12 worlds, then, kindergarten has the tough job of being the equalizer grade to bring children up to speed.

What Kindergarten Looks Like Today

What would Friedrich Froebel think of the twenty-first century kindergarten? I think he would be happy to visit some modern kindergarten classrooms and see that circle time is still the preferred format for reading, singing, large-group demonstrations, and show-and-tell. Of course, circle time now happens on colorful synthetic rugs with shapes, numbers, and alphabet letters, with furniture made of plastic in bright primary colors. In the housekeeping area, toy cell phones and cash registers make electronic beeps. In the refrigerator, the pretend food is multicultural and includes pizza, tacos, sushi, bagels, and eggplant. In the crib, the baby dolls are white, Black, and Asian. On the wall, posters display the alphabet, hand-washing instructions, and class rules that direct children to be respectful. Technology is now part of everyday learning with tablets, digital interactive smart boards, e-books, and educational apps common in classrooms.

Froebel would be impressed but maybe a little disoriented at first. The classroom might feel overstimulating. Froebel might be surprised, but as a progressive thinker, he would understand that a culture socializes its children for the world in which they need to function. Times have changed; the twenty-first century is fast-paced, and its children need to learn to handle different sounds, visuals, and messages to be productive in the world outside of school.

Froebel might be intrigued by the current emphasis on accountability. We assess children with preschool screeners before they come to kindergarten or at the beginning of kindergarten. We test children again at the end of the year to see what they have learned. The issue of assessment is still somewhat confusing for early educators. The 2019 NAEYC position statement *Advancing Equity in Early Childhood Education* calls for assessments to focus on strengths, using authentic assessment methods that provide a well-rounded picture of development. It also makes a strong recommendation that educators recognize their own biases while observing and interpreting children's behaviors and skills.

Froebel might be concerned if he noticed that some kindergarten classrooms do not have toys, dramatic play areas, or blocks. In these spaces, children sit in circle time but do much of their learning with paper worksheets and tablets. He might note that, after all these years, we do not have everything figured out!

Two Kindergarten Classrooms Observed

Like the teachers in *Miss Bindergarten Gets Ready for Kindergarten* (Slate and Wolff 1996), Ms. Gloria and Ms. Susan have spent the last week of August in staff development workshops. They have also prepared their classrooms for students by putting the blocks in their bins, the books on the shelf, and the plastic vegetables in the housekeeping area. The word walls are organized, and the cubbies are labeled.

On the first day of school, twenty children arrive in each classroom, all dressed up, wearing school uniforms and new sneakers. They carry big backpacks on their shoulders. Some children come with their parents, who did not want their children to take the bus on the first day; other children get off the bus a bit tentatively, with name tags on their chests. The youngest children are four and a half years old, admitted through the early-entrance policy, and the oldest are already six years old, having been held back a year because their parents did not think they were ready for kindergarten. Some of the children are just beginning to use full sentences, and a few are already reading on their own.

During the August workshops, the principal of the school where Ms. Gloria and Ms. Susan teach gave a PowerPoint presentation sharing data from the previous year's tests. The school district research and evaluation department has been able to correlate student achievement across four assessments: beginning kindergarten, end of kindergarten, end of first grade, and the third-grade state test. If children meet the benchmarks at each of the first three points, there is a strong probability they will be able to pass the third-grade test in reading and math. The third-grade test is high stakes, as it determines the ranking of the school on the state list. The principal asked teachers to assess the children's learning every month to monitor their progress.

The school district also provided training on language and literacy with specific recommendations for instruction, such as repeated reading, playing phonological awareness games during transitions, holding conversations during small-group times and mealtimes, and engaging parents through simple weekly home activities.

In this magnet school, which attracts families from many parts of the city, the income and education levels of the families are varied, as are the home experiences of the children. Ms. Gloria and Ms. Susan wonder what the year will bring.

Let's see what happens in each of the kindergarten classrooms.

Ms. Gloria

Ms. Gloria's classroom is ready, and the children have arrived. She has been teaching for ten years, and she enjoys her job on most days.

Ms. Gloria found the training interesting, but she feels it is an added imposition. She is upset about all the pressure, but she begins the year by setting her testing schedule. Every first week of the month, a volunteer from the university comes to assess the children. Some students are making good progress, and others are not. Ms. Gloria does not see the point of assessment. She thinks she could have guessed, without the test results, who was doing well—the children whose parents read to them at home and who value education. She has little hope for the others. Ms. Gloria's teaching methods are the same for all children, and she does not see how she could change them. She does not send parents activities to do at home unless parents ask for them at the fall conference.

In this classroom, Ms. Gloria does most of the talking. Children are expected to be silent and obedient, and they spend a lot of time doing worksheets with numbers and letters. The classroom contains puzzles and manipulative toys, but no dramatic play or sensory play options. There is no thematic curriculum. Ms. Gloria says that with all these academics, there is no time left to play.

Ms. Susan

Now, let's visit Ms. Susan's classroom. She teaches down the hall from Ms. Gloria. Ms. Susan has taught in this school for five years. She found the training interesting, and she is curious about how it will work to implement it. She feels the pressure and begins the year by setting her testing schedule. Every first week of the month, a volunteer from the university comes to assess the children. Some students are making good progress, and others are not. Ms. Susan sees the need to put children into small groups to give them more opportunities to practice than they are getting in the large group. Some groups need more help than others to master the skills, so she asks her classroom volunteer to assist. At the fall conference, she explains to all the parents that she is going to start sending home a homework sheet each week, so parents can help their children with numbers and letters. Ms. Susan notes that most parents are following through. As the children's assessments are done monthly, she starts to see overall progress. Ms. Susan believes that assessment helps her do her work better.

In this classroom, children are allowed to wiggle during circle time. Dramatic play is part of the integrated thematic curriculum, with the goal of building vocabulary, an important literacy skill. The more children talk, the better. Each center has reading and writing opportunities, where children can make lists or write letters. Ms. Susan wants children to become familiar with the worksheets they will use in first grade, so occasionally she uses them in her kindergarten class.

Preparing Children for Kindergarten

How then should early educators prepare children for kindergarten? The two scenarios described above are happening, with some variations, in real life. Both scenarios illustrate the point that kindergarten is "all over the place," which might be a bit discouraging; however, this is precisely why it is important for you to be familiar with the kind of kindergarten offered in your community. Early educators should not prepare children for different teaching styles. They should always follow the principles of NAEYC's position on developmentally appropriate practice. At the same time, if preschool teachers have a dialogue with kindergarten teachers, they can do a better job of transitioning children and families.

Discussion Starters

- Reflect on your kindergarten experience. What was it like? What did your parents do or say? What did your teacher do or say?
- What do you believe should happen in a kindergarten classroom? How do these beliefs relate to what you have read in this chapter?
- If you were to meet Ms. Gloria, how would you work with her to begin a plan for the transition to kindergarten?

CHAPTER 3

Preparing Children for Kindergarten

It is a beautiful, sunny day in early August. Julia is climbing on the tall jungle gym at the playground of the elementary school she will attend in September. Her mom, Sara, is enjoying a blissful moment of parental pride. As she looks up from her book, Sara watches her daughter using her feet and hands, in perfect coordination, to get to the highest platform. Sara feels confident that Julia is ready for kindergarten. Not only is Julia sure-footed on the large-muscle equipment, but the nursery school teacher's observations and the preschool screening results were also very reassuring. They confirmed that Julia has all the skills she needs to go to kindergarten. Julia elegantly goes down the slide, but a second later she is running to her mother, crying.

"What's wrong, honey? Did you hurt yourself?" Sara asks.

Julia is sobbing and stomping her feet, "I don't want to go to kindergarten! I am *not* going to kindergarten!"

Sara says, "But, honey, you were so happy about it this morning. And, look, you love the slide here, and you'll have new friends in kindergarten! And your teacher, Ms. Benson, is really nice. You liked her last week when we visited the school!"

After she calms down, Julia is able to explain why she does not want to go to kindergarten anymore. She believes children should know how to read before they start kindergarten, but she does not know how to read yet. She does not feel ready! She asks her mother to teach her to read quickly. Julia's mom gently reminds her that she does not need to know how to read before kindergarten, because she will learn to read in kindergarten and in first grade.

Julia's anxiety is normal. Developmentally at this age, children have good imaginations. They can see things in their minds that are not in the present, and what they imagine may cause them concern. Many children are worried about some aspect of kindergarten. It is a new experience, and they are not always sure it will be as great as other people tell them it will be. The checkout clerk at the supermarket, Julia's church pastor, and her great-aunt Phyllis have already asked her several times when and where she is going to kindergarten. It is part of the social rite of passage for five-year-olds to get a lot of attention about the subject, even from strangers. Some days, Julia responds with enthusiasm and self-confidence. Other times, she feels doubt about her abilities and fear about the unknown. Children have many questions in their heads: Will I find the bathroom? I don't know this teacher. Is she going to be mean? Will she be like my Head Start teacher? The school is so big. Who will find me if I get lost? Do we get to play? I am scared. I don't know the other kids there. I am going to miss my child care. Why do I need to go to kindergarten?

Going to Kindergarten Is a New Situation

Like Julia, children have a wide range of emotions surrounding kindergarten. Sometimes they are excited to be a big kid, and other times they are afraid they will not measure up, or they have misconceptions about what they should know or do. Those emotions are part of the process of adapting to change. First, there is the letting go of the familiar. Julia will be saying goodbye to her preschool teacher, many of her friends, and the routines of her life so far. Then there is the uncertainty of the unknown. Even though she is getting to know her new school and teacher, Julia still is not sure about how it is going to work.

Separation anxiety sometimes appears even if children have previously been away from home in child care. During the preschool years, families usually warn children not to talk to strangers. In a new school, many unknown people—from parents of other students to volunteers to other school staff members—interact with children. Children have to make sense of these contradictory messages.

When adults treat these issues with patience, support, and guidance, children can take control of their feelings and actions to make the change in a positive way. They learn the new rules and places, and they get to trust new people. The result is growth and a sense of self-confidence. In addition to providing early childhood education learning activities, caregivers and parents can also work together to plan special transition activities to facilitate the move from home and preschool to kindergarten.

Teachers, child care providers, and families can prepare children for kindergarten. A solid preparation involves being clear about what children should know by the time they start kindergarten. But children also must adapt to their new kindergarten environment.

Temperament

Leo is always ready for a new adventure. He tries new foods easily, and he is the first one to jump on the merry-go-round at the amusement park. Mathew is cautious in new situations. He asks many questions and wants precise answers. When he is interrupted in his play without warning, he protests loudly and shuts down. Different children have different reactions.

Temperament is the way children are. It is part of their natural dispositions, informing their reactions to events or situations.

Adaptability is one of the temperament traits that affect how children adjust to change (Croft 2021). Some children adapt to new situations fast. Others have more difficulty dealing with change. They are slow to adapt, and they react to any new idea, situation, environment, or person in a negative or cautious way. They need more time and careful preparation to get used to a new experience. Since they don't like surprises, they appreciate knowing what the future holds. To help children who are slow to adapt, it is important to take the time to talk with them about what kindergarten will look, smell, and feel like. Who will be there? What will they wear? What will they do? The more details, the better. Visits to the school to meet the teacher, the principal, and the school nurse are good ways to get children used to the idea and help them understand what will happen and how school works.

Before children get to kindergarten, they need closure with their preschool or child care. It is helpful for them to hear how going to kindergarten will change their schedules and routines, whether they are at home full-time with a parent or attending a child care program. Playing kindergarten is a good activity for children to develop adaptability skills, so they can practice their feelings and actions. Reading books about kindergarten and talking about how the characters feel is also a way to help them process their ideas, providing opportunities to clarify misconceptions like the one Julia had about reading in kindergarten.

Intensity is the second temperament trait that influences children's adjustment to a new situation, as it affects the response like a "driving force" (Kurcinka 2015). Some children have mild reactions when they are anxious or concerned. They become quiet and get teary-eyed when they are upset. Other children cry, scream, and make a scene. These children have intense feelings that may not be worse than what other children feel, but the behaviors are definitely louder. Their intensity is obvious and can cause more stress on teachers and parents. Parents are embarrassed when their child sobs and pulls at their pant legs at the door of the classroom. Teachers do not have the time to calm down the intense child when they have a whole group of children to attend to.

What helps intense children? Try techniques such as reading and telling stories, preparing for the intensity by anticipating beforehand how they will feel, practicing more appropriate behaviors, having sensory activities like playdough to help children relax, or having a quiet area of the classroom to observe the action before being part of it.

Kindergarten teacher Mr. Benjamin notices two children clinging tightly to their parents during orientation. They will not separate from parents during story time, and they want to have parents right with them at the snack table. At the end of the event, when Mr. Benjamin says good-bye, he casually makes the comment that it is sometimes difficult for children to go to kindergarten on the first day because they don't know what to expect. Then he says, "Children, when you come next week, the classroom will be exactly the same. We will have the same yellow playdough on the table and the same fish crackers for snack. I will also read the same book I read today. And if you feel kind of sad, I will not have much time to sit with you, but you can stay in the book corner where it is quiet. You can watch what happens until you are ready to join in." This was a good strategy to help the intense children who need more support for adaptation.

The third consideration regarding temperament is whether the child is more of an *extrovert* or an *introvert*. Introverts get their energy from being alone. Being in a group with many other children and adults in school can be quite difficult for introverts. They tend to need time to think before they speak, and they are not likely to raise their hands easily to volunteer comments. In order to get their space, they may linger quietly in the book or block corner for long periods. Extroverts, on the other hand, get their energy from being with other people. They think aloud and love being the first ones to respond to the teacher's questions. They act friendly. The adjustment to school tends to be easier for extroverts, who know how get attention and connect with others easily. Extroversion is more common and more valued in our society. Introversion is often labeled as shyness and viewed in a more negative light.

Child Development 101: Growth Is Not a Straight Arrow

In chapter 1, we read about what children in this age range can be expected to do. Now I want to draw a brief, typical profile of day-to-day developmental behaviors. You can easily find many developmental checklists in books and on the internet.

It is important to remember that growth does not happen as a straight upward arrow. It is better to visualize growth as an upward spiral. As you follow the movement of the spiral, it goes up and around, then down and around and up again. In the down and around stages, children may not look or feel as competent as they did just a few days earlier. This is part of the normal cycle of physical and mental growth that affects other areas. For example, as the eyes develop and a child gets taller, depth perception changes, so a child who looked very competent going up and down the slide at the park might suddenly freeze at the top, seeming to have lost their skills. The reality is that until the body adjusts again, the bottom of the slide looks much farther away than it did a few days earlier.

Between the ages of four and six, much learning happens, yet it may seem inconsistent. The pattern of growth with periods of equilibrium and disequilibrium, identified in the twentieth century by Arnold Gesell, provides a helpful way to understand children. In addition, theorists like Erikson, Piaget, and Lawrence Kohlberg have given us a valuable foundation from which to interpret child development. They help us understand what general behaviors to expect and why children think and act in predictable ways. Think of the spiral as you read about development.

Physical Development

On average, children between the ages of three and six grow from two to three inches and gain four to six pounds per year. Sleeping, eating, and elimination patterns are established. Permanent teeth appear. The preference for right- or left-handedness is fixed. In order to grow healthy bodies, children need family and school routines that provide a balanced diet, ten to twelve hours of sleep in a twenty-four hour period, and the opportunity to exercise their large and small muscles.

Brain Development

The brain continues to grow until it reaches adult size by the time children are six. The time between birth and six years is a *sensitive* period, during which it is important to provide many opportunities for developing children's intelligence. While it is true that the more stimulation, the better synapses grow and multiply, recent neuroscience research is showing that the brain is more elastic and resilient than we had thought at one time. Children who may not have optimal opportunities to learn at home are not doomed. They can learn in other environments, such as child care and school, and with other adults, such as caregivers and teachers.

Perceptual-Motor Development

Children's perceptual-motor development refers to their ability to move their bodies in relation to other objects they perceive in the environment and to make appropriate accommodations to avoid bumping or overreaching. At the ages of four and five, perceptual-motor development is still evolving. The length of children's arms and legs continues to change as they grow fast. That means large- and small-motor coordination can be inconsistent. Children may be able to write perfect letters one day and not-so-perfect letters the next day as their ability to hold a pencil changes. Children will also reverse letters such as *E* or *F* or *b* or *d* as their vision continues to develop.

Social-Emotional Development

Erik Erikson described children in this age group as being in the *initiative vs. guilt* stage. Children have lots of energy, and they forget their failures and mistakes quickly, which is a good thing because they have a lot to learn and they will make many mistakes in the process. Their imaginations grow with their language and vocabulary. The more words and concepts children have, the more ideas they have in their brains. This leads to fantasies with make-believe stories and tall tales, which in turn can cause guilt and anxieties.

For example, recall earlier in this chapter when Julia imagined she should know how to read before kindergarten. Realizing she was falling short of these self-imposed expectations, she felt anxious. At this stage, if children get the sense from adults that they are bad for their sometimes clumsy attempts and explorations, or if their anxieties are dismissed as trivial, the consequence is a stifling of their sense of initiative. They become afraid to try again. When Julia's mother patiently explains that she is not required to read in kindergarten and expresses her confidence that Julia *will* learn to read in school, Julia learns her abilities are in line with her age. Her sense of competence is then restored.

Moral Development

Kohlberg described children of this age group as being in the preconventional stage of reasoning. Their sense of morality is external. They believe in adages such as "might makes right," "survival of the fittest," and "the strongest one wins." They act based on fear of punishment and desire for reward. For example, children stop their negative behavior when they hear adults use the "countdown" technique of classroom management or when they're promised a sticker for good behavior. They may not quite understand the cause and effect, but they want the sticker. When adults help children use language and everyday situations to examine issues of right and wrong, children learn the tools to progress well into the stage of internal morality, an important skill to regulate behavior.

Cognitive Development

Piaget described children of this age group as being in the preoperational stage. In this stage, children construct their own understandings of concepts and operations (cause and effect, classification, logical reasoning) by actively exploring objects and people. This is especially meaningful when children think about and reflect on what they are doing. They may not have the language to do so, but when adults give children words and help them process their explorations, children learn to use language to represent, remember, and plan things and events. At this stage, children use symbolic play, so they do not have to have the real thing. For example, they use a stick as a gun, or they pretend that a fire needs putting out and use an imaginary hose. Children are egocentric and see the world mostly from their point of view. They are still inefficient in problem solving, but they are always questioning and investigating, so adults can help them think through what they are doing by using open-ended questions and concrete experiences.

Executive Function

Executive function is at the crossroads of cognitive and social-emotional development. These are the abilities that allow children to manage their thoughts, emotions, and behaviors. To be successful in school, children have to learn to control their impulses, take someone else's perspective, communicate to be understood, make connections, take on challenges, and be self-directed and engaged in learning. They learn these skills at home, but perhaps mostly in preschool when teachers introduce games that have rules—like Duck, Duck, Gray Duck; Simon Says; or board games—and sometimes children win and other times they don't. The more children practice with small disappointments and frustrations, like winning or losing during play, the more they strengthen their capacity to overcome the normal challenges of schooling as they grow.

Relating Child Development to Kindergarten Readiness

When thinking about children being ready to go to kindergarten, we should consider where children are on the developmental road. Overall, children are optimistic little creatures, with lots of energy and a desire to learn. When we pay attention to what they need in their classrooms and homes, we give them the best chances to be ready for school. It is not about "pushing down the curriculum"; rather, kindergarten readiness is about being intentional in providing learning opportunities that are concrete and relevant to children's developmental stage. Readiness is about active exploration that mobilizes their bodies and senses to learn early literacy, math, and social skills. It involves providing excellence in all areas of practice (Friedman et al. 2021).

Assessments, Teaching, and Learning

Assessing young children can be controversial. Yet great strides have been made in designing assessments that are developmentally appropriate. Consult the Department of Education of your state for options. Can we assess for "readiness"? Yes, I believe we can and should, using a balanced approach of standardized assessments, parent observations, and teacher observations and evaluations of children's work. The most important part of assessment is using its results as information to teach children. The early learning standards tell us what children should know. Use assessments to find out whether children have the skills to function well in kindergarten, and if they don't, adjust your teaching to ensure they will learn the skills they need by the end of their pre-K year.

Preparing Dual-Language Learners

> *Pablo and Thao are two boys who are four and a half years old. They attend a Head Start program where the instruction is in English. The boys are dual-language learners. Pablo is Latino. His*

parents are immigrants from Guatemala who arrived six months ago. They speak Spanish at home; they do not speak English. Pablo's parents have a second-grade education. Thao is Hmong. His parents speak Hmong and English at home. They came to the United States as refugees ten years ago, when they were in their teens, and they graduated from high school here. Thao was born in the United States. Before entering Head Start, his elderly great-grandparents provided child care for him and his cousins while their parents and grandparents worked. Thao's great-grandparents speak only Hmong.

On a snowy March day, Pablo and Thao are playing with dinosaurs in the block area. Each is holding a dinosaur, and they are facing each other, roaring. "Roar, roar, roar!" They hold their Tyrannosaurus and brontosaurus out and shake them close to each other's face. "Roar, roar, roar!" They smile and are careful not to hurt each other. It is obvious that they like each other and are good buddies. After five minutes, Thao says, "Come, come!" The boys bend down to the floor and begin building a cave for the dinosaurs. To decide on what blocks to use, they show the blocks to each other and nod if they approve, or they say, "Come, come." This cooperative play goes on for another fifteen minutes with no language other than the roaring sounds and "Come, come." The teacher comments that the children do so well playing together that they do not need her to intervene.

Dual-language learners in the United States are children who speak a language other than English at home and who are learning English at school. In other words, they are learning two languages. There are three types of formal educational opportunities for dual-language learners: programs that offer instruction in their home language, bilingual programs with their home language and English, or programs that offer English only as the language of instruction. These options are possible in preschool as well as in elementary school.

In most cases, dual-language learners attend schools where the language of instruction is English. There are two main, practical reasons for this. First, in most areas of the United States, several languages are represented in classrooms, so English is the common language for all. The second reason is that the majority of teachers are monolingual English speakers.

Let's think about Pablo and Thao again. Are they ready for kindergarten? They seem to have the social skills to be in kindergarten. Should we be concerned about their language skills? They will be going to an English-language kindergarten. To be ready for kindergarten, dual-language learners need to have the skills to say what they think, feel, want, and need. That means they should be able to do so as much as possible in English if they are going to attend an English-language kindergarten.

It is a best practice to provide explicit instruction in the dominant language, always in a developmentally appropriate manner, while finding ways to honor and acknowledge each child's cultural and linguistic heritage (Tabors 2008; Passe 2013). Children who are dual-language learners need the following:

- explicit instruction in English, with a strong curriculum that is well integrated so they learn concepts and vocabulary in English
- teaching that builds on children's knowledge of the world from their home languages
- scheduled activities to honor children's home languages, like greetings, book readings, storytelling, and singing
- continuity between home and school cultures, as teachers help parents understand what children are learning in the classroom
- encouraging parents so they continue to speak the home language at home, build concepts, and maintain their cultural connection
- recognition that families have the strength and desire for their children to do well in school

Preparing Children with Special Needs

Marta is six years old. She has Down syndrome. She has been in early childhood special education since she was a baby, first in a home-visiting birth-to-three program, then in a center-based program located in her neighborhood elementary school. Now she is in an inclusion classroom, where there are four special education children and eight mainstream education children. The staff includes a preschool teacher and two assistants. A special education specialist comes every day for two hours to provide extra support. Next year, Marta is going to an inclusion kindergarten.

Marta is gregarious and makes friends easily. She can write an *M*, and she happily puts *M* on everything she paints or scribbles. Her favorite time of the day is active learning when she spends her time in the housekeeping corner, cooking, rocking, and feeding the dolls. She is learning so much in this nurturing and stimulating early childhood classroom that her parents are very nervous about her move to elementary school. They worry that Marta will not have the same level of support and that her growth will slow down. Her parents' concerns can be alleviated with a good plan.

Children who receive special education services need the same consideration and activities as their typically developing peers as they transition to kindergarten. Additionally, children may require the following:

- a coherent plan to avoid overwhelming parents
- a choice of kindergarten placement to meet legal rights, which may be easier in large school districts than in small ones
- information presented in different forms and repeated over a period of time, so as to prevent confusion
- transition-to-kindergarten activities and extra support groups that address their special concerns, such as transportation

Understanding the Kindergarten Teacher's Challenges

Empathy breeds positive actions. I believe it is important for early child-hood educators to understand the challenges of their colleagues, the kindergarten teachers. So here is a glimpse into their reality.

The majority of children adjust readily to kindergarten even as they may have minor discomforts, such as uneasiness in the first few days as they learn about the new school, people, and routines. Another group may experience some problems relating to adjustment and pre-aca-demic preparation. They may know how to share and play with other children, but they may not know how to handle books, listen to a story, or use markers to draw and scribble. The last group, though the small-est, are children whose adjustment is more difficult because they lack the necessary social and pre-academic skills. They may not know how to function in a group setting, have intense separation anxiety, or have a low vocabulary and not know how to express what they want or need. They may be dual-language learners, have special needs that have not been diagnosed, or have a home culture that is so different from the school culture that they feel lost.

If we visualize a real kindergarten class with twenty-five children and one teacher, we can empathize with the challenges kindergarten teachers face. The more early educators prepare children for kindergar-ten, the better they will be able to have a smooth transition.

Whose Job Is It to Prepare Children for Kindergarten?

Parents, pre-K educators, and kindergarten teachers each have a role in helping children transition to school. A winning formula can be achieved when they consider children's temperamental and develop-mental characteristics, as well as the expectations of kindergarten. The first step is to be aware of how the children may react. The second step is to prepare some special activities. All the activities listed in this chapter are good for all children. The children who are less adaptable and more intense may need more time and careful preparation.

What the adults do to prepare children for kindergarten makes the biggest difference in their adjustment to school. Both teachers and parents have an important role. Teachers and caregivers can support children directly and through their work with parents.

"Parents are the child's first teachers" is a common phrase used in most documents and discourse from educators. The original intent is to empower parents so they feel equal in their relationship with teachers. The objective is to ensure that professionals do not take over the functioning of the family. In practice, however, educators are sometimes tempted to blame parents when they do not act according to professional rules and expectations. For example, parents who do not read to their child every night or who do not attend parent-teacher conferences are seen as not caring for their child's education.

Parents or guardians are a child's first teachers for life, and teachers are the first teachers for formal education. This distinction is important in balancing the responsibilities for getting children ready for school. Using health care—another professional field of great value to families—as an example, we could say that parents are children's first doctors when they notice a hot forehead and the child pulling their ears, take the child's temperature, and correctly diagnose an ear infection. They know something is wrong with their child, and they have the good sense that their child needs medical attention. We do not expect them to know the cure.

Families with a low level of education do not have the same skills to talk, read, and write with their children as those with a high level. Parents with a low level of education look to professional educators, who have technical expertise, to teach their children. When these parents say it is the job of the school to teach, it is important to understand and value their perspective. They are already demonstrating a high interest and commitment in education by enrolling their child in a preschool program. Early childhood educators can definitely show parents how reading to children is a good thing. Educators cannot expect that parents will read to their children in the same way, and they cannot accuse parents of failing their parental responsibility, but they can provide them with the tools they need to help their children (just as prevention strategies or a diagnosis, prescriptions for medicine, and instructions on how to give it would be given in the field of health care). Educators need to take a no-fault attitude in order to partner with families most effectively (Melton, Limber, and Teague 1999).

The responsibility for preparing children for school is shared between families, preschool personnel, and kindergarten staff. In the table at the end of this chapter, I propose a way to conceptualize this balance of responsibilities.

Special Transition-to-Kindergarten Activities

Children benefit from specific transition activities that help them prepare for kindergarten. At home, children hear their parents talk about finding a school and registering for kindergarten. In their early childhood classroom or family child care home, children should also have opportunities to talk about kindergarten and play kindergarten so they have an idea of what to expect.

For classrooms and family child care homes with children of mixed ages, toddlers and young preschoolers will have fun, too, playing school and anticipating what they will do in the near future, because they will eventually go to kindergarten. Younger children often make willing "students" for the older children, who will read to them, teach them the alphabet, or have fingerplays. If they are not at all interested, younger children will ignore these activities but do the other fun things you have prepared for them. Telling younger children about their older friends who are going to kindergarten helps to prepare them for their own eventual separation, when they no longer attend your program.

A list of fun, meaningful activities for children who are going into kindergarten within a year follows. The activities are arranged by season, starting with winter, which is when official preparation for school begins, and continuing through summer's end. In the winter, parents attend fairs, visit schools, and make appointments for early childhood screenings and physical checkups. They gather immunization records and birth certificates. Children become aware that all of this activity means a change in their lives is coming. It is also appropriate to introduce the topic of coming change at preschool.

Winter Activities: January, February, and March

❄ *Talk with children about the skills they are learning.*

These conversations can be casual or formal. It is important to tell children that what they are doing before they go to kindergarten will be useful in kindergarten. That way, they can see how the learning they are doing in their classroom, family child care program, or home relates to going to kindergarten. Here is a simple way to explain the concept: "You will be even smarter in kindergarten," or, "You will know how to do it in kindergarten." While this may seem obvious to adults, it is not for children. This knowledge helps them build confidence in themselves as learners and in their abilities to achieve in school. Children's knowledge of their own skills helps them to develop a positive outlook on learning. The skills they are learning include the following:

> learning the names and sounds of letters
> rhyming
> writing letters and their names

listening to and telling stories

counting

singing

sitting in a circle

finishing puzzles

building with large and small blocks

sorting colors and objects

cutting with scissors

painting

gluing

drawing

playing and sharing with friends

talking about what they need, want, and feel

going to the bathroom

washing their hands

dressing and undressing

keeping track of their things

❄ *Develop a portfolio of each child's work.*

Rather than keeping a portfolio as a teacher-only tool, engage the children in collecting samples, which may include drawings, written numbers and letters, photographs of projects, or dictation examples. Talk with children about how much they are learning, and ask them what items they want to add to their portfolios.

❄ *Talk about what is expected and what is not expected in kindergarten.*

Children are expected to sit in circle and listen to storybooks; children are not expected to know how to read. Children are expected to follow their teacher and walk in a line when they go to the lunchroom; children are not expected to find the lunchroom on their own. Having these conversations, which may be conducted in large or small groups, gives children a chance to ask questions and check their assumptions. Like Julia, children may be unnecessarily worried, and they need reassurance.

❄ *Talk about the routines and activities children will do in kindergarten.*

Some routines and activities may be the same as at preschool, and some may be different—playtime; story time; writing; reading; counting; going to the gym, the computer lab, the media center, or the playground; eating in the cafeteria. For children who attend a small family child care, talking about the fact that they will be in school with a big group of children will be helpful. Showing pictures of a kindergarten circle time with twenty children in it will be a good conversation starter.

❄ *Have formal and informal discussions.*

Talk with children about their feelings about change, and share your own feelings. Children should have many opportunities to share their fears and concerns. It is all right to say you will miss them and that you are also proud they are growing up and going to kindergarten.

❄ *Write a class book about children's and teachers' feelings about going to kindergarten.*

After a formal discussion of their feelings about going to kindergarten, children dictate to the teacher how they feel. They can then have their own book and compare it with some of the others they are reading. This is not only a way to teach social-emotional skills but also a meaningful literacy experience.

Spring Activities: April and May

❀ *Invite a kindergarten teacher to visit your program to speak about what happens in kindergarten.*

Sometimes preschool teachers know who the kindergarten teachers are in their community, but sometimes they do not, especially if the school district is large. If this is the case, it may be best for the director of the center to take the first step and connect with the school or schools in the neighborhood. The visiting kindergarten teacher could be a retired teacher who volunteers to visit preschool programs. If you are a family child care provider, contact the local resource and referral network office for ideas. There may already be established connections with the school district or individual schools, or they may know of a colleague who could be a resource. The purpose of this activity is to help children ask questions about kindergarten.

❀ *If you have not yet done so, prepare the children for this visit beforehand by introducing the K-W-L format: what we Know, what we Want to know, and what we have Learned.*

This is a complete literacy activity—with talking, reading, and writing—that can be implemented in a cycle of five days. For the sake of convenience, let's assume a Monday through Friday sequence, but any five-day combination will work.

Monday: Tell the children Ms. X, the kindergarten teacher, will visit on Thursday. Show the K-W-L format, separated into three columns on large easel paper. Tell them you will be using the paper to think and learn about kindergarten.

Tuesday: Ask children what they already know about kindergarten. Write their ideas in the "Know" column.

Wednesday: Review the list of what children know. Ask them what they want to know about kindergarten. Write their ideas in the "Want to know" column. Email the lists to the guest kindergarten teacher, if possible.

Thursday: During the kindergarten teacher's visit, read the questions with the children's help. Facilitate the discussion between children and the guest.

Friday: Ask the children what they have learned about kindergarten. Write their answers in the "Learned" column. Make the connection for children between what they wanted to know and what they have learned.

Leave the chart up for children to refer to on their own or with adult help.

❁ *Have children write a letter about themselves to their kindergarten teacher.*

As the children dictate their words to you, they have to reflect about themselves. This exercise helps them feel proud about themselves as learners and process their ideas and feelings about the future. *Dear Ms./ Mr. ___, My name is ___. These are the things I like to learn about ___. This year, I enjoyed reading ___.* Include drawings.

❁ *Set up a "kindergarten" in the dramatic play area.*

Encourage children to practice being kindergarten students and kindergarten teachers. Ideas for props include books, paper and pencils, stuffed animals and dolls, pointers, an easel with a whiteboard, markers, erasers, an alphabet chart, a calendar, school rules posters, name tags, and a poster of bus rules.

❁ *Show a short video of a kindergarten classroom.*

Some school districts have marketing videos you can obtain, or you could ask someone to record students and teachers in action in a local kindergarten classroom. The recording does not need to be professional quality for the children to enjoy and discuss it. After you've watched the video, talk with the children about what the kindergarten students are doing. Point out similarities and differences between preschool activities and kindergarten activities.

❀ *Read books about kindergarten.*

Some books are about what happens in kindergarten, and many show the mixed emotions of excitement and apprehension that children may identify with. Here are a few books that serve this purpose, and more are available in your local library or bookstore:

Berenstain Bears Go to School, by Stan and Jan Berenstain. The Berenstain Bears are off to school and have many fun adventures.

Kindergarten Rocks!, by Katie Davis. Dexter knows all about kindergarten. His big sister has been there already.

Look Out Kindergarten, Here I Come!, by Nancy Carlson. A family prepares for kindergarten. Henry is excited but also a bit nervous about the new experience.

Making Friends, by Fred Rogers. Children learn about feelings and making friends.

I'm Going to Kindergarten!, by Angèle Sancho Passe. Children and parents get ready for kindergarten with this interactive book, with special tips for parents.

When You Go to Kindergarten, by James Howe. Children go about their day in a kindergarten class.

❀ *Provide opportunities to review the school's website.*

Not only can parents get the information they will need by checking out the school's website, but they can also turn doing so into a literacy activity by viewing it with their children. Some sites include a virtual tour of the school. Be aware that some families may need to be encouraged to access computers at libraries or community centers.

Summer Activities: June, July, and August

✲ *Play on the school playground, which is open to children for play outside of school hours and during the summer.*

Children can get used to being on school property. The familiarity also gives them a sense of ownership of *their* school. When they learn to use the ladders, slides, and tunnels, children develop a sense of competence.

✲ *Send children to summer school kindergarten camp during July or August, if available.*

As part of their summer school program, some school districts offer Kinder Kamps. The length varies from one or two days to six weeks. Typically, one or more kindergarten teachers run these kindergarten camps. The teachers get to know the children, and the children get a formal introduction to the school. They learn the routines of arrival, meals, circle time, free play, learning centers, storybook reading, and dismissal. Fees and transportation depend on the budget. In some districts, the program is at no cost and includes busing. In others, families pay a fee and transport their children. If children have a difficult time separating, parents may stay with them and gradually leave.

✲ *Attend the school picnic before school opens.*

The week before school starts, or right after, many schools offer picnics with principals, teachers, school secretaries, classroom assistants, and other school staff, including cafeteria workers, nurses, and bus drivers. This is a fun opportunity for parents, children, and school personnel to meet, eat together, and tour the school.

✪ *Attend a kindergarten "play date" before school starts.*

Some schools organize a playground party in August after the class lists are finalized. Children from each class get to know one another and play in the schoolyard.

✪ *Participate in bus safety workshops for children and parents to learn the rules of the bus.*

The workshops often include a presentation by a bus driver or representative of the transportation department, a tour of the bus, and in some cases a short drive around the block. Parents can ask questions about safety and the logistics of the bus schedule.

This list of transition-to-kindergarten activities is quite long, so choose the ones that appeal to you most or those you are not currently doing. The idea is to be intentional in the ways you prepare children.

Discussion Starters

- Think of two children you know and remember how they each react to change. What feelings are the children experiencing? What do their reactions look like? What helps each child cope best?
- Preparing children for kindergarten can be formal or informal. What would be examples of each? What approach do you use in your own program?
- What activities will you do in your program to make children ready for kindergarten? What do you need to implement them? Draft a schedule with three activities you can implement for winter, spring, and summer.

ARE CHILDREN READY FOR KINDERGARTEN?

Children are ready for kindergarten when they have the following developmentally appropriate skills, which allow them to function in school:

They have the language to say what they think, want, feel, and need.

They get along with children and adults.

They understand their own feelings and the feelings of others.

They have pre-academic knowledge of vocabulary and conversation, phonology, and concepts of print and math including knowledge of the alphabet and numbers.

They use scribbling, writing, and drawing to represent and interpret ideas.

They see themselves as learners and approach learning with curiosity and interest.

They use their imaginations to play and create ideas and objects.

They take care of their physical needs (toileting, dressing).

They use school tools (puzzles, scissors, computers, pencils, markers).

They move their bodies, legs, and arms with coordination.

They transition between activities with ease.

They persist at several tasks throughout the day.

They function well in groups, sharing ideas, toys, materials, and space.

They follow two- and three-step directions.

They sit and participate in circle time and small groups.

They understand they are going to a new school called *kindergarten*.

What Children Need to Be Ready for and to Succeed in Kindergarten	Family Responsibility	Preschool Program or Family Child Care Responsibility	Kindergarten Responsibility
Physical health	Shelter, food, clothes, safety, and a healthy lifestyle, including family routines that respect sleep	A safe, clean learning environment Information to families on child growth and development	A safe, clean learning environment
Strong early literacy and language skills	Opportunities for talking and reading in the home language Ongoing learning experiences at home	Language- and literacy-rich curriculum Intentional instruction in English or the home language Activities for parents to do at home that are related to what children are learning in the classroom	Language- and literacy-rich curriculum Intentional instruction in English or the home language Ideas for parents to do at home that are related to what children are learning in the classroom
Strong social and emotional skills	Love, nurturance, positive discipline	Positive environment Respect for and acknowledgment of diversity	A positive environment Respect for and acknowledgment of diversity
Positive attitude toward learning	A supporting role in children's education Space and time for learning Encouragement of curiosity	High, developmentally appropriate expectations to encourage and challenge children	High, developmentally appropriate expectations to encourage and challenge children Information for families on helping children to be academically successful

What Children Need to Be Ready for and to Succeed in Kindergarten	Family Responsibility	Preschool Program or Family Child Care Responsibility	Kindergarten Responsibility
Special activities to adjust to kindergarten	Talking, reading, and writing related to kindergarten Participation in activities offered by the preschool and kindergarten Completion of the required registration procedures in a timely manner	Talking, reading, and writing related to kindergarten Inclusion of transition activities in the preschool curriculum	Opportunities for learning about kindergarten
A warm welcome	Support for the children through adjustments to the new school	A positive send-off to kindergarten	A simple process for registering Inclusion of preschool routines and books in the curriculum Welcoming activities: (an open house, an introduction-to-kindergarten mini-camp, a welcome letter) Activities provided on a flexible schedule
Families working with the school as partners	Use of positive strategies to collaborate with the school	Training and support for parents to learn how to participate and have meaningful roles	Training and support for parents to learn how to participate and have meaningful roles Activities provided for families on a flexible schedule
Families supported by the community	Knowing where and how to find community resources	Providing access to support services that enhance the formal education of children (health care, cultural events)	Providing access to support services that enhance the formal education of children (health care, cultural events)

CHAPTER 4

Preparing Families for Kindergarten

Sally is a family child care provider. Emma, the oldest child in her care, is going to kindergarten next year. Since she was a baby, Emma has been with Sally. Sally is sad to see Emma go to kindergarten, but she is proud too. This is the first child graduating from her licensed home, which she started five years ago. When she talks about Emma's parents, however, Sally just shakes her head. "They are just a wreck," she says. "They have a choice of two schools, and they are so nervous about picking the right one. Sometimes they don't sleep at night. They are always asking me questions. What should I tell them? I try to reassure them that Emma will do fine, but . . ."

In the life cycle of families, going to kindergarten is a milestone, just like the birth of a child five years earlier, and high school graduation twelve years later. Even if children have been in a child care setting or preschool, this is the first time parents feel they are handing their child over to the big, mysterious institution of education.

When I ask participants in workshops to remember kindergarten, they usually have vivid memories. Sometimes they remember it as a happy time of excitement and discovery, sometimes as a sad feeling of being left in a strange place with people they did not know, unsure of what to expect. The experience somewhat depends on the person's per-sonality. Some children adapt more easily than others to new situations; the same goes for parents. Some parents feel confident the elementary school is a good place for their child. Others feel more anxious and uncertain about whether the school will meet the needs of their child.

A Road Map to Kindergarten

What do parents need to know about kindergarten? Maybe we should first ask what parents *want* to know—an important distinction, if we are going to be sensitive to their needs. Parents' hopes and concerns are the business of preschool educators who are caring for their children. When we work with a child, we are working with their family too (Keyser 2017). Having a strong caregiver-family partnership is particularly beneficial in facilitating the readiness of children and the transition to kindergarten—for all children but especially those in poverty (Brooks-Gunn 2008).

In some communities, like large school districts that offer school choices, the entrance to kindergarten can be complicated. Parents are expected to attend school fairs as early as November, visit schools during December and January, and make their preference known to the enrollment office by the middle of February. This means that parents have to be proactive and well organized, and in many cases, their child has not even turned five yet! With only their own memories of kinder-garten and the advice of friends and neighbors, parents navigating the system for the first time do not have a road map to the new kindergarten. Many things have changed in the last two or three decades in education. It has become a more technical field, with professional jargon, rules, and expectations. So even well-educated parents feel anxious.

Families' Hopes

On the first day of kindergarten, I volunteered to be a community greeter at a school in Minneapolis. My job was to be near the entrance greeting children and parents and directing them to the right classroom if they seemed lost. I saw many beautiful children holding their parents' hands or getting off the buses by themselves. Some had confident steps, and others looked more tentative. Many children were wearing sparkling new clothes and carrying colorful new backpacks. Their parents had probably taken their pictures that morning for family scrapbooks.

Six types of school, family, and community involvement have been identified by Joyce Epstein at Johns Hopkins University: parenting, communicating, volunteering, learning at home, decision-making, and collaborating with the community (Epstein et al. 2018). *Parenting* relates to the work that families do to provide for the health and safety of children as well as to maintain a home environment that encourages learning and good behavior in school. Parenting means making sure children are well fed, rested, and dressed; have good manners; and know how to get along with others.

When parents send children to school in their finery, they want educators to notice they are good parents because they take good care of their children. Parents also hope that if their children look good teachers will have a better impression of their family and will teach their children better. This thinking may be an intuitive response, as teachers really do tend to have lower opinions about children from families they perceive as disorganized (Arce 2019).

After more than one hundred years of existence, kindergarten is a normal part of our culture. Parents see kindergarten as the beginning of children's educational career. Parents want the best for their children, and they can learn how education works.

Families' Anxieties

As part of a school readiness project in a large urban district, I conducted focus groups with parents to find out what they thought about school readiness, as well as to learn their anxieties and expectations about the entrance to kindergarten.

"Frankly, my biggest fear is the ride in the bus," said Ann, the mother of a four-year-old who was going to kindergarten next year. "You just hear so much bad stuff about the older kids misbehaving and the bus driver not being able to handle it." The thought of leaving a fresh-faced five-year-old on a big school bus with fifty-nine other students, ranging from kindergartners to eighth graders, is scary, especially when children have to be at the bus stop during hours when it's still dark in the morning.

In addition to bus safety, parents worry about the emotional safety of their children at school. Many questions come to their minds: Will the teacher like my child? Will my child make friends? What if my child is bullied? Who will protect my child and discipline the bully? Will my child learn things in school that are against our beliefs or religion? Parents may also be anxious about the scary effects of active shooter drills.

Parents also want to know about the academic expectations of kindergarten, which teacher their child will have, and the placement of their child in a particular classroom. These concerns are practical and have concrete answers that will help parents visualize what their child will be doing and with whom. Having the answers relieves their anxieties and helps parents prepare their child at home for the transition.

Addressing Families' Feelings and Needs

Families want opportunities to meet the school staff and know other families. They are looking for practical tips on how to prepare their children for school. Transition activities such as kindergarten orientation reassure them that the school will provide a quality experience and make sure their student succeeds through timely, regular, respectful, and confidential communication. So let's facilitate this for them.

Families have the right to be involved in their child's education at school in ways that are most important to them. For example, the following is a list drafted by one district's parent advisory council as a families' bill of rights to illustrate what is important to parents:

- feeling welcomed at school, with a variety of opportunities for involvement
- providing timely, regular, respectful, and confidential communication in a variety of formats (in person, written, electronic, video)
- prioritizing safety in school, on the bus, on the playground, and during school-related activities, such as field trips
- demonstrating culturally sensitive respect from school staff
- accessing information and decision-making staff, who can provide information and solve problems in the school and the district

The importance of family engagement is clear in the official guidance of Head Start, as every program is mandated to have a transition plan (US Department of Health and Human Services 2018). Family participation in the transition to kindergarten is a key element of school readiness. The same is required of the programs participating in QRIS programs across the nation.

Helping Families Prepare Children

Immigrant families, families facing poverty, and families with low educational levels may not be familiar with the culture of education, and they may not know how to conduct a school search. They expect that the preschool program and school system will guide them to the best options for their children.

In a Hmong parents' focus group, Pheng, a father of five, offered his thoughts. "I want to say that you go about it the wrong way. Your parenting programs' brochures say, 'Come to our program to be a better parent.' But we are already good parents! It should say, 'Come to our program to make your child a better student.'" The other participants nod in approval at Pheng's boldness, laughing. They repeat for emphasis, "That is the wrong way! We need to know more about education and how to help our children learn in school, not how to take care of them!" They are right. We have to spread this message now.

Let's look again at Epstein's types of family involvement, including parenting, communicating, volunteering, learning at home, decision-making, and collaborating with the community. These categories, commonly adopted by the K–12 system, describe what parents need to know. While educators have focused their efforts on the parenting and learning at home categories, it seems that parents would like to know more about the other types of involvement.

Parenting

Parenting is what parents do every day. They need confirmation about how important their job is to the education of their children by making the connection between home and school explicit. The following are some examples of how parenting ties into education:

- Taking care of the physical needs of children (food, shelter, clothing) helps children grow physically healthy and be ready to learn. When children are rested, they can better attend to what the teacher is teaching. Their brains are more ready to learn.
- When they have the right clothing—such as a coat, boots, and mittens in cold climates—children can play in the schoolyard safely. And having had good, healthy exercise, children can be better learners when they return to the classroom.
- Teaching children at home about manners, right and wrong, and discipline also teaches them to get along with other children and adults in school.

Communicating

Schools have peculiar methods of communication that may not be immediately obvious to families. Teachers should let parents know how their communication works:

- The backpack plays a primary role in distributing communication. The school newsletter and teacher's notes go home in the child's backpack, and parents need to check it every day.
- Report cards are distributed to families two to four times a year. They contain information about how children are progressing in school, especially in different subject areas such as reading and math. The report card also gives parents a sense of their child's behavior. Show parents how to read the information on a report card and talk about what it all means.
- Parent-teacher conferences are typically held in the fall and spring. Conferences usually have a set schedule. Teachers often send home a sign-up sheet for conference times (in the backpack) that parents are expected to return, or sign-up happens online. Conferences can last between ten and twenty minutes. If more time is needed, parents may request an additional meeting with the teacher, but the meeting cannot usually go over the time scheduled on conference day, out of respect for the other parents waiting in line. Pre-K educators can practice parent-teacher conferences and give parents tips on what questions to ask and how to be the best advocate for their child.
- Parents need to know that they can contact their child's teacher in person or by texts or emails. Teachers are often too busy to have a long conversation at drop-off and pickup times, but these are good times to set future appointments. Many classrooms have secure electronic web pages or use communication apps for easy contact too.

Volunteering

Parents are encouraged to volunteer to help the school. The children, staff, and school benefit from the extra assistance. Some volunteer work may be done at school or even at home, such as preparing art materials or making phone calls. At the beginning of the school year, many schools give parents a questionnaire that asks them how they would like to volunteer. Even if they don't return the questionnaire, parents need to know they are welcome to volunteer at any time. Some volunteer opportunities include:

- tutoring small groups or individual learners in the classroom in subjects including literacy, math, science, or languages
- preparing materials for art projects or filling backpacks with the weekly news
- supervising a small group of children on field trips
- working in the office, assisting the secretary with making photocopies or preparing mailings
- raising funds for a school project or requesting donations from businesses
- coaching a sport or a club

Learning at Home

This area is about helping parents understand that they can support the job of the school at home with specific actions. Learning at home refers mostly to doing early literacy activities in the course of daily life. Talking and having conversations about everyday events, reading books, telling stories, counting socks while folding the laundry, drawing, and writing are all examples of learning at home. Doing these activities at home reinforces their learning at school:

- cooking, sewing, painting, and writing letters to relatives, which help children become better students by showing them how to apply what they're learning in school in everyday life

- making sure children do the homework assigned by the teacher, such as looking for items that start with the same letter—oranges, olives, and oatmeal
- making room at the kitchen table or in a quiet corner for reading and studying
- turning off the television so there are more opportunities to interact and fewer distractions when children are doing their homework
- limiting the use of electronic tools and media, which are known to lower attention spans and increase irritability and acting out
- spending family time outdoors, such as playing at a park or walking through the neighborhood

Decision-Making

In addition, families can choose to be involved in decision-making for the school, for example by participating in a Parent Teacher Organization (PTO) or joining budget or staffing committees. When Head Start centers, public preschools, and private nonprofit programs invite families on their governing boards, families gain valuable experience. It prepares them well for future involvement in their children's education in the school system.

Collaborating with the Community

Schools have increased the services they provide to families beyond education, including social services, dental clinics, and health check-ups for children, and adult education such as language or parenting classes.

Six Reassuring Messages

All in all, preparing families for kindergarten requires educators to pay attention to how they explain the culture of their field without assuming what parents already know. I see teachers who are discouraged when they plan an elaborate event for families and few show up. They blame the weather or a lack of parental interest; yet other teachers consistently have good attendance and response from families. The message makes a difference. The more direct teachers are, the more they can reach parents effectively. I have categorized six messages from educators that reassure families as they visualize themselves as partners in education, beginning in the preschool years, and as children progress into elementary school.

Message 1: Families and Educators Will Work Together to Teach Children

Common literacy-building activities that help children learn at home and at school are talking, reading, writing, and learning new things. The common social skills and behavioral activities are getting along, sharing, respecting each other, learning self-control, and practicing safety.

When parents do activities at home that are similar to what teachers are doing in their classrooms, children do better in school. Then the culture of home and the culture of school are in line. In fact, individual families can express their culture in unique ways. For example, literacy activities at home can just as easily involve reading the Bible or the Koran as reading fairy tales or magazines. Talking about what to have for dinner, whether it's tacos or pizza, is useful for the development of children's vocabulary. Once families understand this concept, they feel validated and supported in the activities they do with their children, which also helps instill in their children the importance of learning. It provides them with concrete examples of a true family-school partnership.

Message 2: Educators Will Help Children Learn Academic Subjects at School

When I take my car to the mechanics, I expect they will be the expert on advising me as to what my car needs. On my last visit for routine maintenance, I was given a list of potential preventive actions I could take and the puzzling choice of which ones I wanted. If I did all of them, the cost would be out of my budget. I was totally overwhelmed. When I asked which ones were most important, the mechanic only said that they were all recommended and it would be my *personal* choice. He kept repeating that he was not forcing me to do anything; he was just giving me the list of my options. I left there confused and irritated. I wondered if this mechanic had just attended a training workshop on car-owner involvement. He wanted me to be involved in the maintenance of my own car; however, he was missing a very crucial point: I lacked the information and the confidence to make a decision. His approach was not helping me.

Sometimes, I am afraid we do that with families. We want them to be involved in their child's academic learning, but we expect them to have more background information than they do. When we ask parents to read to their children at home, for example, we may be putting unreasonable demands on them if they cannot read. So when talking with parents about their involvement, we need to ask them first what their ideas are. Then we can reassure them that we will provide the best education we can because we are the experts in education.

Message 3: Educators Will Tell Families What "Ready for Kindergarten" Means

Parents need to understand what skills children should be learning in preschool in order to be ready for kindergarten. These skills are based on the early learning standards provided in chapter 1. The standards, however, may be too technical for parents to understand without explanation.

The "Are Children Ready for Kindergarten?" list in chapter 3 and in appendix B is more concrete and easier for parents to apply. I recommend you use it as a guide in your conferences with parents or as a basis for handouts and newsletter articles.

Message 4: Families Will Need to Help the Kindergarten Teacher Know Their Child

Families can feel intimidated by the formality of elementary schools and may be hesitant to approach their child's kindergarten teacher. They need encouragement from pre-K educators to accept the invitations of the school and feel more confident in helping the kindergarten teacher know their child. Some ways to do so include:

- visiting the school
- meeting the principal and the teacher
- sharing the child's preschool portfolio
- learning how to stay in touch with the teacher with a card or an email, whether they are concerned or satisfied

Message 5: Families Will Play a Special Role in Helping Their Child Become a Good Student

Kindergarten teachers express concerns that children come to school tired or dressed inappropriately for the weather or an activity. Sometimes their attendance is sporadic. These concerns are legitimate, as they diminish the ability of students to pay attention or function well in school. Here are some guidelines for parents, who want to be told explicitly what their role in this area is to help children become good students:

- When children are well rested and well fed, it is easier for them to concentrate and learn.
- When children have warm clothes during cold-weather months, they can go outside for recess and play.

- Sometimes children wear party clothes to school but then worry they will get them dirty. When children wear durable, easy-to-wash clothes, they can do potentially messy activities, such as painting or playing in the sand.
- Children who are in school every day learn more and have better test scores than those whose attendance is sporadic.
- Reading every day helps children become better students.
- Children who watch a lot of television at home do not do as well in school as those who play and read books.

Message 6: Kindergarten Will Be a New Experience for All Children

Some children will be excited and happy about going to kindergarten, while other children will be nervous and worried. Some children show excitement on the first day but want to stay home the next day. That's normal. It does not mean the first day was traumatic, only that the novelty of school has already worn off. The transition to kindergarten goes better when parents help children adjust by being sensitive to their concerns and talking about them. Children need gentle but firm encouragement.

Special Transition Activities to Prepare Families for Kindergarten

At the same time families are preparing their children for kindergarten, you can take measures to prepare families for kindergarten. Here is a list of activities for you to use with the parents of children in your care who are soon going to kindergarten:

Explain to families how your classroom activities help children get ready for school.

How classroom activities help children is not always obvious to parents. When I was an administrator, I was once called by one of my teachers to observe a parenting group for Hmong parents. The parents had been giggling throughout circle time and would not sing along, which frustrated the teacher. When I arrived, I saw seven moms sitting in a circle with their preschool children, the teacher, and a Hmong interpreter. The teacher started singing "Five Little Ducks." A few seconds into the song, the mothers started giggling, and the teacher looked at me with discouragement. At the end of the session, the teacher and I talked about the purpose of singing "Five Little Ducks." Without hesitation, she told me the children were learning about counting and separation (the baby ducks go out to play, away from their mother, who calls them back, one by one, to the end). The children were also sitting in a circle, just like they would soon do in kindergarten, and they were learning some English words. It made perfect sense to the teacher that this song had educational value.

Then I asked the teacher if she thought the parents knew the purpose of singing "Five Little Ducks." She was perplexed. After all, why wouldn't they? Then she smiled, realizing the mothers probably didn't know. The following week, she asked the interpreter to explain to the parents why the song was important. The parents listened attentively, asked questions, and nodded with serious interest when they were told about the song's educational value—and there were no more disruptive giggles. The parents participated eagerly because, of course, they too wanted their children to learn. From then on, the teacher explained the learning objectives of each activity, enriching the parents' understanding.

Provide parents with good feedback on how their children are learning in your early childhood program.

Parents want to know not only how their children are behaving but also which early literacy skills their children are acquiring. This feedback will answer parents' questions about whether their child is ready for kindergarten and will give them confidence in their child's abilities. Parents will then also have appropriate language to describe their child's readiness for kindergarten to the new teacher.

Teach parents how to use portfolios with the kindergarten teacher.

Prepare children's portfolios to share with parents. Each portfolio should include assessment results, which demonstrate knowledge of letters, sounds, and numbers. It should also include writing and drawing samples, as well as dictations that explain a drawing or a story. Pictures of the child playing cooperatively in the dramatic play area or showing a structure they created in the block area are also nice to have. These illustrations help parents and kindergarten teachers visualize the child's learning.

Use parent-child activity books to anticipate the start of kindergarten.

Consider books such as *I'm Going to Kindergarten!* (Passe 2013), which is an interactive book I created for parents and children to talk about themselves and what they will do in kindergarten.

Offer parent workshops that promote learning activities at home.

It is important to teach parents, especially those with low educational levels, how to ask their children open-ended questions and to play what-if games, as well as to encourage them to talk, read, and write with their children.

Distribute information to parents about school choices.

Help parents learn how the process for choosing a school works and how to find the deadlines for registration. Often, registration materials are written at a high level, which can make them difficult for some parents to read. You may offer to help read the materials, explaining some of the words if need be.

Encourage parents to attend open houses and orientation sessions at their child's new elementary school.

Most elementary schools offer open houses and orientation sessions where families are invited to tour the school and meet the staff. Some schools include the children, while others do not. Many of these events are held in the evenings, though some have day and afternoon options. Sometimes families are shy about attending, worried that they will not know anyone, or they may not understand the purpose of it as the official welcome to kindergarten. They are more likely to attend if a preschool provider encourages them directly.

Invite school district representatives to your center or family child care home to discuss kindergarten with parents.

Parents trust you and will feel reassured about meeting elementary school staff in the familiar setting of your program. Your presence at these workshops is an added bonus as parents know they can count on you to help clarify information that is confusing.

Education, with its jargon and research findings, is a complicated business for those outside of it. We on the inside tend to forget ever having to learn the meanings of words and concepts like *social-emotional, cognitive, physical development, approaches to learning,* and *early literacy skills,* and we talk without interpreting those meanings for noneducators. Jargon can be a problem for parents, and those who aren't used to it can find it confusing or annoying.

A simple glossary of terms and abbreviations frequently used by educators follows. (You may wish to add to the list other terms and abbreviations that are frequently used in your area.) A list such as this one is helpful not only for parents in general but also for interpreters who translate for parents who do not speak English.

TERMS

approaches to learning: How children become curious about learning new things and how they think about what they have learned.

child development: What we know from the areas of child psychology, medicine, and education about how children grow.

cognitive development: How children learn to think, make decisions, and solve problems.

language and literacy development: How children learn to listen, speak, read, and write.

physical and motor development: How children use their growing bodies to make large movements with their legs and arms (gross-motor movements) and to make small movements with their fingers and hands (fine-motor movements); children learn coordination and control of their gross-motor movements when they run, climb, or ride a tricycle; they learn coordination and control of their fine-motor movements when they cut with scissors, use a pencil, or assemble a Lego toy.

self-regulation: How children increase their ability to control their feelings and their bodies so they can behave well; for example, if a child wants to share a toy, the child asks to use it rather than simply grabbing it.

social and emotional development: How children learn about feelings, both their own and those of others.

social skills: The abilities that children learn in order to play with others, share, sit in groups, wait their turns, get along with other children and adults, and follow rules.

ABBREVIATIONS

BOE (board of education): A group of elected officials who oversee the work of a school district.

DLL (dual-language learner): A student who is learning a home language and English at the same time.

DOE (Department of Education): The US federal government and each state government have special offices that provide guidance and funding for education.

ESSA (Every Student Succeeds Act): The national policy that holds K–12 public schools accountable for providing quality education for all children.

FERPA (Family Educational Rights and Privacy Act): The law that ensures the privacy of students' records regarding grades and behavior.

FTE (full-time equivalent): Describes the assignment of school personnel; for example, a kindergarten teacher may teach two half-day sessions as a full-time employee, or 1.0 FTE.

IDEA (Individuals with Disabilities Education Act): The law that ensures services to children with disabilities throughout the United States. Part C covers children ages birth to two years, and part B covers children ages three to twenty-one years.

IEP (individualized education program): A learning plan for children who receive special education services.

K–12 (kindergarten through grade twelve): Describes the school system. Increasingly, school districts are adopting the term pre-K–12, demonstrating their commitment to preschool as part of the educational continuum.

PTA (Parent Teacher Association): A parent-run board that supports the work of school staff; a school's PTA is a member of the National Parent Teacher Association.

PTO (Parent Teacher Organization): A parent-run board that supports the work of school staff; a school's PTO operates independently and is not a member of the National Parent Teacher Association.

SEL (social-emotional learning): The process of developing the self-awareness, self-control, and interpersonal skills that are necessary for school, work, and life success.

STEM (science, technology, engineering, mathematics): Skills and mindsets that can be taught to prepare children for the problem-solving needs of our technological future.

TA (teaching assistant): Sometimes referred to as an EA (educational assistant), this employee is a paraprofessional who assists teachers in the classroom. Some kindergarten classrooms have a TA, but most do not.

I chose a few of the most common terms and abbreviations used in early learning standards documents and parent newsletters, and I was reminded how unclear we can be in our communication with families. For example, if the teacher says, "Lisa has good social skills," Lisa's dad might smile but leave wondering exactly what the teacher meant. On the other hand, if the teacher says, "Lisa plays well with her classmates, really does a good job of waiting her turn, and is firm but polite when she asks for what she needs," her dad will have a much better idea of Lisa's "social skills."

ARE FAMILIES READY FOR KINDERGARTEN?

Families are ready for kindergarten when they understand their role as partners in the education of their child, when they know what to do at home to prepare their child for kindergarten, and when they follow the procedures for orientation and registration:

They prepare their child for kindergarten by providing opportunities at home for the child to talk, read, and write.

They provide opportunities for their child to experience high-quality group settings.

They follow procedures for preschool screening and school choice.

They choose a school that fits their family's needs.

They complete the registration for kindergarten in a timely manner.

They attend informational events and workshops.

They follow through on referrals to other agencies, such as for a special education assessment or social services.

They visit schools.

They meet the school's kindergarten teachers and principal.

They attend school orientations and events.

They talk with their child about kindergarten.

They use the information they receive to reassure and prepare their child for the transition from home and preschool to kindergarten.

They begin to develop a plan for being involved in their child's elementary school education.

Discussion Starters

- Think of the families in your child care center or family child care home whose children will be going to kindergarten soon. What are they saying or doing? What does that mean for your work with them?
- Review the list of key messages families benefit from hearing. Which ones do you feel confident giving to parents? Which ones do you need to practice more?
- What activities will you offer families to help them and their children be ready for kindergarten? What do you need in order to implement the activities? Draw up a schedule with three ideas you can do for winter, spring, and summer. Find ideas in the booklet *Getting Ready for Kindergarten*, especially written for families.

CHAPTER 5

Preparing Early Educators

Carmen is a family child care provider. She has been doing this work for the past ten years. Carmen has a diverse group of children ranging in ages from six months to five years. Some children are Latino and speak Spanish at home, and other children are Anglo and are learning Spanish in her care. Through her local resource and referral network, she enrolled in a special early literacy project that provides her with materials, a rich curriculum, and a literacy coach who visits her every other week. "This has changed my life," she says proudly. "I am much more intentional about what I teach the children because now I know what they need to learn. Before, I didn't!" She enthusiastically names the fun and interesting activities that are integrated with the books she is reading: rhyming, playing restaurant or veterinary clinic in dramatic play, singing and pointing to the alphabet, and playing bingo games with numbers. Now Carmen does not worry that children will write on the walls because she has set up a writing center. Her children are more engaged in learning, and as a result, they are also better behaved—quite a bonus for everyone!

Next fall, three of the children—Mona, Luis, and Amy—are going to kindergarten. They are all firstborns, so it is a new experience for their parents, who are quite excited and nervous at the

*same time. They love Carmen and are sad to leave her. Carmen is
sad, too, but she wants to make sure the children are well prepared
for kindergarten. With the help of her coach, she designs a transition-to-kindergarten plan for the children and their families.*

*Carmen attended workshops offered by the community school
on how to facilitate the transition of children and their families to
kindergarten. At the workshops, she learned three things: she has
an important role in preparing children for kindergarten; focusing on early literacy and social-emotional skills will help the children become ready for kindergarten; and for parents who are new
to sending their children to kindergarten, she is a guide to the culture of education. Carmen already knew she was important to the
children as the person who cared for them and loved them when
their parents were at work. She now has a new awareness about
the value of her job. She has become more knowledgeable about
the expectations of kindergarten so she can teach the children. She
can also work closely with parents because she has learned about
the enrollment and registration procedures in her school district.*

Early Educators' Roles

Much of what happens in a preschool classroom, family child care
home, or parent-education group serving families with four- and five-
year-olds is, of course, preparing them for kindergarten at some level. In
my observations over the years, however, that preparation has tended to
be rather superficial with some general encouragement and individual
problem solving, but not necessarily with intentional actions.

When I talk to groups of early educators, I am surprised by how many
of them have opinions or judgments about the kindergartens in their
communities. Then, after they express their opinions, I find out how few
have actually visited these classrooms or interacted with teachers and
principals. The teachers make comments, such as, "I don't want to talk

with parents about kindergarten because I think the kindergartens in our area are not good," or, "When parents ask me for advice, I am afraid to get caught in the middle." These comments make me nervous. I want to propose some actions to encourage and empower early educators to prepare themselves and to work with kindergartens to do a better job of preparing children and families. Kindergarten is their business too.

All Who Care for Children Are Teachers

First, let's clarify who cares for children. From the parents' point of view, anyone who cares for their children has a caring *and* teaching role. Parents use the word *school* when they talk about child care. In general, they have two main goals for child care: a safe, healthy environment and school readiness. Based on licensing rules, preschool programs and family child care homes follow standards for health and safety first. They are increasing their focus on social-emotional skills and language and literacy skills with the addition of STEM (science, technology, engineering, mathematics), or even STEAM, with *A* standing for "arts." The demands on the curriculum for early childhood education have steadily become more rigorous.

Just before Mother's Day, Mona and Luis are at the writing center. On the table, there are envelopes, an assortment of cards in different designs, pencils, and crayons. The children decide to make cards for their moms, following Carmen's earlier suggestion. They are selecting their cards when Amy joins them. Now, all three are busily drawing, writing, and coloring. Mona is writing a succession of unrelated letters. They are well formed and in clusters but do not yet make words. When she finishes, she looks at her card very pensively for a long time. Finally she shows it to Luis and says, "I don't remember what I wrote. Can you read it to me?" Luis studies the card carefully and replies confidently, "It says, 'I love you,

Mommy!"' Amy looks up from her own work and smiles. "I am writing 'I love you, Mommy' too!"

This beautiful scene does not happen by accident. It is the result of an intentional educator. It tells us that the family child care provider, Carmen, is planning materials and activities to stimulate children's learning so they are ready for kindergarten. When children grow and learn in a literacy-rich environment, interplay like that among Mona, Luis, and Amy occurs. When children do not get opportunities to learn, the behaviors that stimulate their educational growth are missing. It is encouraging to see the national efforts for increasing quality in early education having an effect in settings like this one.

Practical Tools for Gauging Early Literacy Behaviors

Sometimes I worry that we rely on the "hope theory" of education—we *hope* they learn! It is a risky attitude when we don't know for sure which actions to take so the children *do* learn. Observing and then analyzing our observations is a good way to gauge if what we hope is happening is indeed happening. I propose that early childhood educators use two charts to assess the literacy richness of their own classrooms or homes. These charts are not evaluation instruments. They are tools to develop awareness, and they can be used for discussion. The first chart is for observing children in your program and making note of what you see. It is best to use it over a period of two to three days so there are more occasions in which to see different scenarios and behaviors. You'll record in the "Often," "Sometimes," and "Never" columns the initials of the children as you see them doing the things listed. The second chart is for making observations of the adults in your program (including yourself!). Use it in the same manner—for a few days—and in the columns for "Often," "Sometimes," and "Never," write the initials of the teachers as you see them engaging in the practices listed.

Literacy-Richness Assessment #1: Children's Behaviors

OBSERVE CHILDREN TALKING, READING, AND WRITING
THROUGHOUT THE DAY

In Our Classroom or Child Care Home, We See . . .	*Often*	*Sometimes*	*Never*
Children talking to each other while playing (free play or small group), while eating at the snack or lunch table, and while transitioning (to the bathroom, cleaning up, or waiting for the bus).			
Children talking to the adults, initiating and engaging them in conversation.			
Children responding to adults with language and gestures.			
Children using multiple-word sentences in English, in their home language, or in both.			
Children "reading" or looking at picture books independently or with other children.			
Children listening to, understanding, and talking about the stories when adults read to them.			
Children scribbling or writing in an age-appropriate manner.			
Children asking questions to gather information and extend their learning.			
Children singing.			
Children listening to and following directions with more than one step from adults.			
Children talking about and drawing their activities and ideas.			
Children dictating their ideas to adults.			
Children counting and using early math concepts independently or with other children.			

If you *often* observe children performing these activities, feel confident they are on the road to being ready to learn in kindergarten. If the results are *sometimes* or *never*, then increase those learning opportunities for children. Plan activities that are interesting to the children so they practice more talking, reading, and writing during their time in your care instead of, for example, only at circle time. Remember that children learn best through play and hands-on experiences.

Literacy-Richness Assessment #2: Adults' Behaviors

OBSERVE ADULTS TALKING, READING, AND WRITING WITH
THE CHILDREN

In Our Classroom or Child Care Home, We See . . .	*Often*	*Sometimes*	*Never*
Adults reading to children in a large group.			
Adults reading to individual children or small groups of children.			
Adults engaging children in conversation while reading (dialogic reading).			
Adults asking questions that expand learning and vocabulary (ask: *how, what, when, who*).			
Adults writing down ideas dictated to them by children.			
Adults listening to children.			
Adults responding to children's questions.			
Adults facilitating play by offering verbal descriptions and suggestions to expand play and vocabulary.			
Adults talking with children during transitions.			
Adults giving verbal directions.			
Adults promoting conversation during meal times.			

In Our Classroom or Child Care Home, We See . . .	*Often*	*Sometimes*	*Never*
Adults playing language games (rhyming, making up silly names and sounds, counting) with children.			
Adults using encouraging words and signs (*yes, good, try again, smile,* and *thumbs up*).			
Adults affirming children for being learners.			
Adults leading discussions about stories after reading a book.			
Adults teaching letters and sounds in English and in other languages, as appropriate.			
Adults teaching numbers and early math concepts in English and in other languages, as appropriate.			
English-speaking adults speaking and reading English with children learning English, using gestures as appropriate.			
English-speaking adults teaching English words and sentences to children learning English.			
Adults honoring children's home languages and culture with greetings, songs, books, and visitors, as appropriate.			

If you *often* observe yourself and other adults performing these activities, congratulations! You are doing a great job of intentionally promoting language and early literacy skills. If the results are *sometimes* or *never,* be concerned that the early education provided may not be of a consistent quality. Connect with your local child care resource and referral (CCR&R) agency, join your local chapter of NAEYC, or take a class. Often, small grants are available for teachers and family child care providers to improve their skills or to buy teaching materials for the purpose of increasing their quality of work.

Providing Feedback to Parents

Parents need to get meaningful feedback about their children's learning so they can work with educators in tandem. In focus groups, parents say they want to know about their children's development and what they need to learn to be ready for kindergarten. Rather than providing general comments, it is best when educators are specific. Examples of what early educators say and what parents want and need to hear follow:

What Educators Say	What Parents Want and Need to Hear
Omar is doing so well!	Omar will be ready to learn to read in kindergarten. He has a good vocabulary for his age, and he understands the sounds of English. These are two important pre-reading skills.
Sara likes to play with other children in the housekeeping area.	When Sara plays in the housekeeping area, she shares toys and negotiates with other children. These are good social skills to have in kindergarten.
Michael knows six letters of the alphabet.	Michael knows six letters of the alphabet. To be ready for kindergarten, research says it is better if he knows about fourteen to sixteen letters. We are working on this at school. Here are some ideas to do at home.
Mona can write her name.	Mona can write her name. She is ready to do that in kindergarten.
Thao is using more English now.	Thao speaks English with me and the other children to tell us what he wants and how he feels. I know he understands the stories by his answers to my questions, which will help him get ready for kindergarten.
Marian does not listen well to directions.	We are teaching Marian to listen to directions. In kindergarten, there is only one teacher, so it is important for Marian to learn this skill. I'll tell you what we do at school to help Marian learn to listen better, and let's think about what you can do at home to help as well.

Parents want to know how what their child is doing in preschool will help them be successful in kindergarten. Even though children's progress may be obvious for early educators, it is not always so for parents.

Early Childhood Educators Learn about Kindergarten

Early childhood educators develop strong and trusting relationships with families. Parents often see educators twice a day, and they share intimate stories of their lives at home. They look to educators for guidance in the education of their child. Parents go through their own separation anxiety when their child is moving on to the big next step of kindergarten. They may ask questions about kindergarten that a preschool teacher or family child care provider cannot answer if they are unfamiliar with what goes on in kindergarten.

In my work, I often hear pre-K educators say, "Kindergarten is not my business." Or I hear them say they don't like what is happening in kindergarten, usually implying that the schooling is not developmentally appropriate, so they try to avoid the topic. I'd like to encourage you to make it your business to know about the kindergartens in your community. This will help you be more informed so you can pass on the information to parents. It will also help you better understand the system you are preparing children for. If, indeed, you do not agree with what happens in kindergarten, you will be able to advocate for better methods after you are more knowledgeable.

You need to have good information and a connection with kindergarten staff to better prepare children. Here are some suggestions to help you become more knowledgeable about the kindergartens in your community:

- Visit one or two schools children might attend. That will give you a sense of what happens in an elementary school.
- Spend some time—one hour is enough—in a kindergarten classroom so you can see what children do as well as what is expected of them.

- Attend school district informational events or explore the district website to learn more about kindergarten expectations.
- Become familiar with the registration process so you can guide families through it. You do not have to become an expert, but you need to know where or whom to refer them to. Distribute materials about kindergarten registration to families.
- Invite kindergarten teachers and principals to visit your program and tell them what you do to prepare children and parents for kindergarten. Show them examples of students' work, the parent newsletter, the curriculum, and the daily schedule you follow in teaching children. Kindergarten teachers who understand the educational practices of early childhood programs see children in a more positive light.
- If your local school district does not have a transition plan, take the initiative. Develop one yourself! Involve school staff. You can advise elementary schools on how to best serve the families you know so well. The next chapter provides information on how to pull the transition plan together.

Discussion Starters

- Use the literacy-richness assessment charts for children's behaviors and for adults' behaviors and assess your home or classroom. What do you see? What needs to change? How will you make these changes?
- What educators say may be different from what parents want and need to hear about their child's learning. Reflect on the words you use when you talk with parents. Can you rephrase them to be more specific about how a child's skills or behaviors relate to being ready for kindergarten?

ARE EARLY EDUCATORS READY TO PREPARE CHILDREN FOR KINDERGARTEN?

Early educators are ready to prepare children for kindergarten when they intentionally include the transition to kindergarten in their curricula and teaching practices:

- They teach intentionally to develop the early literacy and social-emotional skills of all children.

- They provide feedback to parents on children's overall development and early literacy skills.

- They use a consistent portfolio of children's work and duplicate it for parents to share with kindergarten teachers.

- They provide early literacy workshops for parents.

- They promote home-learning activities.

- They invite kindergarten teachers and principals to visit their programs.

- They familiarize children with kindergarten classroom rituals.

- They stay informed of the expectations of kindergartens in their communities.

- They visit kindergarten classrooms.

- They distribute information about kindergarten to their families.

- They support parents through the school choice and registration process.

- They train parents to be advocates for their children.

CHAPTER 6

Transition-to-Kindergarten Planning

Mary is a new Head Start pre-K teacher in a small rural town. Next year, most of the children in her classroom are going to kindergarten. She realizes she has not been in a kindergarten classroom since her own children were in school, about fifteen years ago. Mary wants to visit a kindergarten and talk with the kindergarten teacher to get ideas about how to prepare the children now. She calls the elementary school to schedule an observation and is pleasantly surprised by the warm reception. It's an all-day kindergarten, and Mary decides to observe in the morning. Her director supports her efforts and finds a substitute for the duration.

Mary enjoys observing the kindergarten class and is intrigued to see how much writing the children are doing. She takes pictures to show her children what kindergarten looks like. As she leaves, the teacher gives her a handout titled What Children Should Know before Kindergarten. She also offers Mary her phone number and asks her to call with any questions. Over the next few weeks, the two of them continue to communicate. Mary is grateful for the tips the kindergarten teacher gives her. She incorporates some of the ideas into her curriculum and shares others with parents. She talks to her director and colleagues about her experience.

They decide to design a comprehensive plan for the transition to kindergarten so all children and families can benefit.

Whose responsibility is it to lead the transition-to-kindergarten work? Ideally, the responsibility is shared between the sending preschool program and the receiving school. Someone, however, has to lead. In some places, elementary schools take the lead because they have concerns about the readiness of children coming in. In other communities, preschool programs take the lead because they want to help families feel more comfortable about the transition to kindergarten. Often, the leadership comes from an enterprising center director, preschool teacher, principal, or kindergarten teacher who calls a few people and says, "How about getting together to figure out how to make the transition to kindergarten smoother?" If you have such an idea in your head, or if a colleague has approached you about it, what follows are tools for doing just that.

Continuity Is the Goal

The goal of planning the transition to kindergarten is to provide continuity for children and families. Change is stressful. New routines can be confusing. Continuity is reassuring. The more children and parents understand about what will come next, the easier it will be for them to ready themselves for the new situation rather than just worrying about it. For children, opportunities for continuity include the books that they will read in both their pre-K setting and kindergarten, the activities they will be provided, and the songs they will sing. For families, opportunities for continuity include the paperwork they will be asked to complete, the events or routines they will be able to participate in, and the services they will be able to access. When preschool and kindergarten teachers and administrators are familiar with each other's settings, they are better able to prepare children and families for change.

Thinking about Logistics

Now that you have a good understanding of what children, families, and staff need, it is time to consider the organizational structure of planning the transition to kindergarten. Organizational structure will vary based on location. The process and size of the planning project will be different in a large school district than in a small one. The number of people to involve, amount of money to budget, and logistics required to organize it all depend on the nature of the specific situation. The planning may be easier to do in a smaller district, compact in geography, where working relationships among professionals have already been established. In larger school districts, it may be more practical for professionals to divide into groups by neighborhood rather than trying to cover the entire geographic area.

The most important step is the first one: Start! Begin! Get going! If no one in your community has broached the subject, be the leader! Planning the transition is a necessary service to all families and an especially important one for families who need extra support to understand the educational system. You, as an early childhood professional, can contribute to real systemic change beyond the scope of your child care home, classroom, or center as well as to the overall success of children and families.

Pre-K to K–12 Collaboration

Preschool programs and elementary schools should work together to plan and implement the transition to kindergarten. In some communities, you can take advantage of existing "Pre-K–3" (preschool to third grade) alignment efforts (Stipek et al. 2017). In these districts, there is an intentional effort to bridge preschool and elementary education. In other areas, you may have to initiate the collaboration. With a decentralized early childhood system and many school choice options for families, the web can be complicated. For elementary schools, there may be less urgency to plan for the transition because, ready or not, children and families will show up every year at the appointed time. For preschool programs, however, hearing parents' anxieties over the transition is an incentive to do something to make it easier. I strongly recommend that preschool programs take the initiative to develop a transition-to-kindergarten team. The team's first meeting may be the most challenging to organize; rest assured, it will get easier after that.

Start small and follow a simple framework to begin. Starting small is okay, and success is more likely later on. Here are the components of a simple process in six easy steps:

1. Convene a transition-to-kindergarten team, involving colleagues from early childhood, elementary schools, and parents.
2. Follow a strategic plan.
3. Choose transition-to-kindergarten activities.
4. Decide on actions needed to implement the transition-to-kindergarten strategies, including resources such as money, materials, people, and time.
5. Implement the actions.
6. Evaluate the successfulness of the plan.

Let's begin planning!

Convene a transition-to-kindergarten team, involving colleagues from early childhood, elementary schools, and parents.

Recruiting participants is the first step. Reach out to other professionals on both sides of kindergarten—pre-K teachers, family child care providers, child care center directors, kindergarten teachers, principals, and school secretaries. Invite them to a meeting to discuss the transition to kindergarten. This transition team will probably need to meet four or five times.

Whether the meeting is in person or by video conference, make it friendly for people who have been working all day, and allow them to think in a relaxed atmosphere. Explain the purpose of the meeting, using information from this book as your rationale. Invite three or four pre-K parents and kindergarten parents to the subsequent meetings. Ideally, the transition team should consist of eight to ten people, a size that makes facilitating and building relationships more manageable. The last task of this first meeting is to schedule the next meeting.

Follow a strategic plan.

This is the overall map for the transition. In the table that follows, I have listed the best transition-to-kindergarten strategies discussed in this book. The strategies are arranged according to the academic year. With some exceptions, such as in school districts that follow year-round schedules, school business is mostly seasonal, with events occurring in a predictable pattern in fall, winter, spring, and summer. Most schools' calendars run from September to June.

Notice that responsibility is shared for some strategies and not for others. Defining responsibilities makes the overall implementation of the strategies easier to execute, because each group can focus on the portions of the plan for which it is responsible. A blank strategic plan is available for your use in appendix E, and a downloadable version is also posted at www.redleafpress. org. Type "ready for kindergarten" in the search box and follow the links.

www.redleafpress
.org/rfk/app-e.pdf

Transition-to-Kindergarten Strategic Plan

Transition-to-Kindergarten Strategy	Responsibility	Schedule
Get staff ready to prepare children and families for kindergarten through training and planning activities.	Pre-K and elementary teachers	Fall Winter
Get families ready for kindergarten through special transition activities.	Pre-K teachers, providers, and parent educators	Winter Spring
Get children ready for kindergarten through instructional learning activities and special transition activities.	Pre-K teachers and providers	Fall Winter Spring
Welcome children and families to kindergarten.	Kindergarten teachers and principals	Spring Summer Fall of kindergarten year

Choose transition-to-kindergarten activities.

Once you have your strategic plan to guide you, decide which transition-to-kindergarten activities you want to offer children and families. Review the suggestions for:

    activities to prepare children (in chapter 3)
    activities to prepare families (in chapter 4)
    activities to prepare staff (in chapter 5)

As you discuss the activities with your colleagues on the transition team, think about transition activities you are already doing and some you would like to add. Start small and choose one or two activities for each strategy.

Decide on actions needed to implement the transition-to-kindergarten activities, including resources such as money, materials, people, and time.

After you have chosen the transition-to-kindergarten activities, you have to think carefully about how to make them a reality. The success of your strategic plan will depend on how thoroughly and realistically you realize and manage the resources needed to implement your actions. Good ideas and enthusiasm are not enough! You have to consider the money, environment, people, and materials needed, and the deadlines and leadership required. A blank transition-to-kindergarten action planning chart is available for your use in appendix F.

www.redleafpress
.org/rfk/app-f.pdf

Example Action Plan for Transition-to-Kindergarten Activities

Transition Strategy	Transition Activity	Actions to Be Taken	Person Responsible	Resources Needed (Money, Space, People, Materials)	Dates
Get children ready for kindergarten.	Set up a "play kindergarten" theme in the preschool room.	Set up kindergarten play in the dramatic play area. Find books about kindergarten at the library. Write a note to parents in the newsletter about the transition to kindergarten.	Preschool teacher and assistant	Books about kindergarten; easel, markers, and a pointer; alphabet chart; dolls and stuffed animals to be "students." No extra money or space are needed.	April 15 to May 9
	End the kindergarten theme with a visit from a kindergarten teacher.	Invite a retired kindergarten teacher to visit the classroom. Prepare children for the visit using K-W-L.	Preschool teacher	Camera to take pictures; cost of chocolate candy to thank the kindergarten teacher	May 5
Get families ready for kindergarten.	Provide parent workshops about child development and expectations for kindergarten.	Recruit a speaker from a parent-education program. Reserve the room. Copy handouts.	Center director	Speaker's fees; refreshments cost; meeting room: no cost	January 15

Implement the actions.

You are now ready to carry out the plan. Keep in mind the overall goal of making the transition to kindergarten smooth for children and families. You may have to make adjustments if the people involved or the resources change.

Evaluate the success of the plan.

Evaluate your plan and actions. Take good notes during the implementation and evaluation meetings so you can refer to them when you prepare the transition to kindergarten for the following year. Use the following questions for your evaluation:
- What aspects went well and why?
- What aspects need improvement and how can improvements be made?
- What is not worth repeating and why?

Yes, a Good Transition to Kindergarten Can Happen!

At a meeting of experts who were designing a professional development system for early childhood educators, the first questions to arise were "Are children ready for school?" and "Are schools ready for children and families?" The discussion was passionate. I understood why the participants were preoccupied with the issues—we must keep addressing the critical and fundamental idea of school readiness. We must continue to pay attention to the readiness of children and the readiness of schools at the same time and to look for solutions in both areas. Debating the relative value of each is not necessary. They are both critically important. The goal is to make a really good connection between preschool and elementary education so children, families, and educators have solid continuity.

There are two wonderful parts to my job: observing children learn and watching early educators teach. The anecdotes in this book are from real situations, and two more follow. The first shows how the quality of instruction helps children learn pre-academic skills in a play setting. The second demonstrates how thoughtful transition activities facilitate the adjustment of children to the new experience of entering kindergarten.

As you read, reflect on how the early learning standards are applied and how children are getting ready for kindergarten with the support of adults.

Children Learning through Play

In a small rural town on a winter day, it is too cold to play outdoors. The pre-K teacher, Ms. S, sees her children are bursting with energy, and, as usual, she dreads letting them loose in the big gym, which her school readiness program shares with the high school. This time, she comes prepared with her "literacy bucket," which contains strips of paper, small notebooks, markers, pencils, tape, stickers, three-by-five index cards, play money, and scissors.

In the gym, she pulls balls, a basketball hoop, tractors, tricycles, and a toy gas pump out of a closet. Immediately, children begin to use the large-motor equipment to tear across the gym at top speed, creating safety chaos. Ms. S sets up three play learning centers—a gas station, a basketball court, and a parking lot near the basketball court. She engages the children in setting speed limits, and they post the signs around the room. Then Ms. S begins to issue fines to the drivers who go above the speed limit. Soon, not only is the traffic madness manageable, but the children are also busy buying and selling gasoline, signing checks and using credit cards, making driver's licenses, counting money, reading signs, and keeping track of the basketball scores. These children are learning the skills to be ready for kindergarten.

Kindergarten Is Okay

Clara is not so sure she wants to go to kindergarten next year. So much talk about it is making her nervous. She does not like new situations.

When Jeanine, her family child care provider, sets up a kindergarten classroom in her basement dramatic play area, Clara ignores it for a whole week. Jeanine and Clara's parents know Clara's temperament well, so they slowly present her with stories, comments, and opportunities to get used to the idea of kindergarten. Eventually, Clara begins to play kindergarten, as the teacher to the stuffed animals. Sometimes she is mean and yells at them, especially when they don't seem to follow her directions. Other times, she is sweet and sensitive, imitating her provider's nurturing style.

Jeanine teaches Clara preliteracy skills. They read interesting books, have extended conversations, sing rhyming songs, write letters, and paint. There is a lot of time for play. With her parents, Clara visits the new school, climbs on the school playground, and attends a kindergarten roundup. Since she is the only four-year-old in Jeanine's small family child care home, her parents sign her up for the three-week Kinder Kamp in July that is offered by the school. At Kinder Kamp, Clara learns about being part of a large group of children and practices the kindergarten routines.

On the first day of kindergarten, Clara clings tightly to her mother at first. She slowly lets go to participate in the classroom activities. When her mother picks her up and asks her about her day, Clara smiles and says quietly, "Kindergarten is okay."

A Few Last Words

We can clearly answer the question "Is everybody ready for kindergarten?" when we understand that "everybody" does not apply to just children. Kindergarten is everybody's business: parents, early childhood professionals, and elementary school teachers and principals. When adults understand each other and work together, they do a better job of helping children adjust to school, and children have better early literacy skills and are better prepared for reading. Children also have better social-emotional skills, allowing them to get along with other children and adults as well as to succeed in the social group setting of school. Everyone benefits.

Over the years, I have talked to many early childhood educators, parents, children, kindergarten teachers, and school principals and have discovered a good thing: the transition to kindergarten is smooth for many children and families, thanks to the efforts of countless education professionals around the country. When you read this book, I hope you confirm that the work you already do to prepare children and families is on the right track. I also hope that you feel a great confidence to continue your good work. Last, when you read this book, I hope your creativity is sparked and new ideas for your program come to you and make your job easier.

In the short term, we need to take a practical approach to getting all children ready for kindergarten. Simple activities performed regularly will lead to more complex systemic changes over time.

Over the long term, we must remain alert to our practices: it is imperative that excellent developmentally and culturally appropriate practices are always used in the teaching of all children and in the welcoming of all families. We can accomplish this together by being the best pre-K educators we can and by collaborating with our K–12 colleagues. Together, we can make sure everybody is ready for kindergarten.

Discussion Starters

- Review the steps for planning the transition to kindergarten. Which steps have you already started? What would you need to do next?
- What are the barriers and opportunities to collaborating with elementary schools in your community? Make a list of each. How can you use the opportunities to overcome some of the barriers? Who do you need to talk to?

- Now that you have finished the book, review chapters 3, 4, 5, and 6 and make notes about the areas in which you are already doing well. Examine the areas in which you would like to put more effort to improve the transition to kindergarten.

Resources

The following online resources are intended to be helpful to you in your work as you look for ideas, examples, and research related to the transition to kindergarten.

Center for Inclusive Child Care (CICC)
www.inclusivechildcare.org

    The CICC provides free relationship-based professional development including support, training, and modeling to programs in Minnesota. In addition, the CICC website has an extensive library of resources for early educators around the United States, particularly in social-emotional learning and strategies for behavior guidance.

Centers for Disease Control and Prevention (CDC) Developmental Milestones Resources
www.cdc.gov/ncbddd/actearly/milestones/index.html

    The developmental milestones (in English and Spanish) offer families and educators checklists, videos, and recommendations to track and support child development from birth to five years. While the checklists are not validated tests, they are practical tools for further observations and assessment of young children.

Child Care Aware of America (CCAoA)
www.childcareaware.org

    CCAoA works as a national network of more than four hundred child care resource and referral (CCR&R) agencies and other partners to provide comprehensive information about quality child care, state by state. The website offers detailed tools, including each state's version of its early learning standards and indicators of progress.

Childhood Education International (CE International)
www.ceinternational1892.org

    CE International is a membership organization started in 1892 by kindergarten educators. It provides an international perspective on the field of early childhood

From *Ready for Kindergarten* by Angèle Sancho Passe, © 2023. Redleaf Press grants permission to photocopy this page for classroom and child care home use.

education, developing resources such as the *International Principles of Practice for Educators.*

Head Start: Early Childhood Learning and Knowledge Center
https://eclkc.ohs.acf.hhs.gov

The Head Start website offers information and tips for parents, staff, and administrators on all aspects of early childhood education, including the transition to kindergarten. Handouts can be duplicated to give to families or to train staff.

Illinois Early Learning (IEL) Project
www.illinoisearlylearning.org

The IEL Project website has information on early care and education for parents, caregivers, and teachers of young children. The resources are relevant to all who are interested in early childhood issues. The website offers printable tip sheets for educators and parents in English and other languages.

National Association for the Education of Young Children (NAEYC)
www.naeyc.org

NAEYC is the largest membership association for the early childhood education profession, with affiliates in most states and members worldwide. Its mission is to improve the well-being of all young children from birth to age eight, through the quality of early childhood programs, teachers, and caregivers. NAEYC does seminal work on developmentally appropriate practice, ethics, professionalism, diversity and equity, authentic assessment, and technology.

National Black Child Development Institute (NBCDI)
www.nbcdi.org

NBCDI focuses on the well-being and early education of Black children ages zero to eight years with a cultural competence lens. It serves as a national resource agency, supplying programs, publications, advocacy, and training.

National Center for Cultural Competence (NCCC)

http://nccc.georgetown.edu

NCCC is part of the Center for Child and Human Development at Georgetown University. It provides training, technical assistance, and consulting to promote and sustain cultural and linguistic competency.

National Center for Learning Disabilities (NCLD)

www.ncld.org

NCLD provides information and promotes research on effective learning. One of NCLD's related websites is GetReadytoRead.org, which contains a special section on the transition to kindergarten, with tools and resources focused on early literacy skills.

National Institute for Early Education Research (NIEER)

https://nieer.org

NIEER conducts and communicates research to support high-quality, effective early childhood education for all young children. The website offers practical information and reports on a wide range of education and policy topics. It also provides access to other national and international resources.

Pyramid Model Consortium

www.pyramidmodel.org

The Pyramid Model posits that children need a gradational approach with guidance to learn social-emotional competence. At the base, all children build relationships in supportive environments and interactions. Going higher on the pyramid, some children need extra teaching support. Then, at the top, a small group of children need additional support in the form of individualized interventions.

Teaching for Change

www.teachingforchange.org

Teaching for Change offers professional development, lessons, and resources to help classroom teachers supplement their pre-K–12 curricula. The website has a section on early childhood anti-bias education.

United Nations Educational, Scientific, and Cultural Organization (UNESCO)

www.unesco.org

UNESCO is the educational, scientific, and cultural branch of the United Nations. As such, it focuses on the rights of young children to care, education, and health at the policy level. UNESCO's Global Partnership Strategy for Early Childhood 2021–2030 expresses the goal of ensuring that early childhood education, development, and investment services are fully inclusive, accessible, affordable, gender-responsive, and equitable for each child. This website provides an international perspective.

Are Children Ready for Kindergarten? Checklist

Children are ready for kindergarten when they have the following developmentally appropriate skills, which allow them to function in school.

☐ They have the language to say what they think, want, feel, and need.

☐ They get along with other children and adults.

☐ They understand their own feelings and the feelings of others.

☐ They have pre-academic knowledge of vocabulary and conversation, phonology, and concepts of print and math including the alphabet and numbers.

☐ They use scribbling, writing, and drawing to represent and interpret ideas.

☐ They see themselves as learners and approach learning with curiosity and interest.

☐ They use their imaginations to play and create ideas and objects.

☐ They take care of their physical needs (toileting, dressing).

☐ They use school tools (puzzles, scissors, computers, pencils, markers).

☐ They move their bodies, legs, and arms with coordination.

☐ They transition between activities with ease.

☐ They persist at several tasks throughout the day.

☐ They function well in groups, sharing ideas, toys, materials, and space.

☐ They follow two- and three-step directions.

☐ They sit and participate in circle time and small groups.

☐ They understand they are going to a new school called *kindergarten*.

From *Ready for Kindergarten* by Angèle Sancho Passe, © 2023. Redleaf Press grants permission to photocopy this page for classroom and child care home use.

Are Families Ready for Kindergarten? Checklist

Families are ready for kindergarten when they understand their role as partners in the education of their child, when they know what to do at home to prepare their child for kindergarten, and when they follow the procedures for orientation and registration.

☐ They prepare their child for kindergarten by providing opportunities at home for their child to talk, read, and write.

☐ They provide opportunities for their child to experience high-quality group settings.

☐ They follow procedures for preschool screening and school choice.

☐ They choose a school that fits their family's needs.

☐ They complete the registration for kindergarten in a timely manner.

☐ They attend informational events and workshops.

☐ They follow through on referrals to other agencies, such as for a special education assessment or social services.

☐ They visit schools.

☐ They meet the school's kindergarten teacher and principal.

☐ They attend school orientations and events.

☐ They talk with their child about kindergarten.

☐ They use the information they receive to reassure and prepare their child for the transition from home and preschool to kindergarten.

☐ They begin to develop a plan for being involved in their child's elementary school education.

From *Ready for Kindergarten* by Angèle Sancho Passe, © 2023. Redleaf Press grants permission to photocopy this page for classroom and child care home use.

Are Early Educators Ready to Prepare Children for Kindergarten? Checklist

Pre-K teachers, family child care providers, and family educators are ready to prepare children for kindergarten when they intentionally include the transition to kindergarten in their curricula and teaching practices.

- ☐ They teach intentionally to develop the early literacy and social-emotional skills of all children.

- ☐ They provide feedback to parents on children's overall development and early literacy skills.

- ☐ They use a consistent portfolio of children's work and duplicate it for parents to share with kindergarten teachers.

- ☐ They provide early literacy workshops for parents.

- ☐ They promote home-learning activities.

- ☐ They invite kindergarten teachers and principals to visit their programs.

- ☐ They familiarize children with kindergarten classroom rituals.

- ☐ They stay informed of the expectations of kindergartens in their communities.

- ☐ They visit kindergarten classrooms.

- ☐ They distribute information about kindergarten to their families.

- ☐ They support parents through the school choice and registration process.

- ☐ They train parents to be advocates for their children.

From *Ready for Kindergarten* by Angèle Sancho Passe, © 2023. Redleaf Press grants permission to photocopy this page for classroom and child care home use.

Transition to Kindergarten Strategic Plan Template

TRANSITION-TO-KINDERGARTEN STRATEGY	RESPONSIBILITY	SCHEDULE

From *Ready for Kindergarten* by Angèle Sancho Passe, © 2023. Redleaf Press grants permission to photocopy this page for classroom and child care home use.

Action Plan for Transition-to-Kindergarten Activities Template

Transition Strategy	Transition Activity	Actions to Be Taken	Person Responsible	Resources Needed (Money, Space, People, Materials)	Dates

From *Ready for Kindergarten* by Angèle Sancho Passe, © 2023. Redleaf Press grants permission to photocopy this page for classroom and child care home use.

References

Abry, Tashia, Scott Latham, Daphna Bassok, and Jennifer LoCasale-Crouch. 2015. "Preschool and Kindergarten Teachers' Beliefs about Early School Competencies: Misalignment Matters for Kindergarten Adjustment." *Early Childhood Research Quarterly* 31 (2): 78–88.

Annie E. Casey Foundation. n.d. "Kids Count Data Center." Accessed January 20, 2021. https://datacenter.kidscount.org.

Arce, Samantha. 2019. "Exploring Parent and Teacher Perceptions of Family Engagement." *International Journal of Teacher Leadership* 10 (2): 82–94.

Brooks-Gunn, Jeanne. 2008. "Reducing Gaps in School Readiness: Education, Health, and Parenting Strategies." Lecture presented at the McEvoy Lecture Series on Early Childhood and Public Policy at the University of Minnesota, Minneapolis.

Brooks-Gunn, Jeanne, Cecilia Elena Rouse, and Sara McLanahan. 2007. "Racial and Ethnic Gaps in School Readiness." In *School Readiness and the Transition to Kindergarten in the Era of Accountability,* eds. Robert C. Pianta, Martha J. Cox, and Kyle L. Snow, 283–305. Baltimore: Paul H. Brookes.

Campbell, Coral, Chris Speldewinde, Christine Howitt, and Amy MacDonald. 2018. "STEM Practice in the Early Years." *Creative Education* 9 (1): 11–25.

Christenson, Sandra L. 1999. "Families and Schools: Rights, Responsibilities, Resources, and Relationships." In *The Transition to Kindergarten,* eds. Robert C. Pianta and Martha J. Cox, 143–77. Baltimore: Paul H. Brookes.

Croft, Cindy. 2021. *Why Temperament Matters: Guidance Strategies for Young Children.* St. Paul, MN: Redleaf Press.

Delpit, Lisa. 1995. *Other People's Children: Cultural Conflict in the Classroom.* New York: The New Press.

Derman-Sparks, Louise, Julie Olsen Edwards, and Catherine Goins. 2020. *Anti-Bias Education for Young Children and Ourselves.* 2nd ed. Washington, DC: NAEYC.

Doucet, Fabienne, and Jonathan Tudge. 2007. "Co-constructing the Transition to School: Reframing the Novice versus Expert Roles of Children, Parents, and Teachers from a Cultural Perspective." In *School Readiness and the Transition to Kindergarten in the Era of Accountability,* eds. Robert C. Pianta, Martha J. Cox, and Kyle L. Snow, 307–38. Baltimore: Paul H. Brookes.

Dunckley, Victoria. L. 2015. *Reset Your Child's Brain: A Four-Week Plan to End Meltdowns, Raise Grades, and Boost Social Skills by Reversing the Effects of Electronic Screen-Time.* Novato, CA: New World Library.

Durkin, Kelley, Mark W. Lipsey, Dale C. Farran, and Sarah E. Wiesen. 2022. "Effects of a Statewide Pre-kindergarten Program on Children's Achievement and Behavior through Sixth Grade." *Developmental Psychology* 58 (3): 470–84.

Early Care and Education Crisis Work Group. 2023 Legislative Priorities. https://d2a9ofpqdihxfr.cloudfront.net/wp-content/uploads/2023/02/Leg.-Priorities-1-23-23.pdf.

Ehrlich, Stacy B., Kyle DeMeo Cook, Dana Thomson, Kristie Kauerz, Mitchell R. Barrows, Tamara Halle, Molly F. Gordon, Margaret Soli, Andrew Schaper, Sarah Her, and Gabriella Guerra. 2021. *Understanding Cross-Systems Transitions from Head Start to Kindergarten: A Review of the Knowledge Base and a Theory of Change.* Washington, DC: Office of Planning, Research, and Evaluation.

Epstein, Joyce L., Mavis G. Sanders, Steven B. Sheldon, Beth S. Simon, Karen Clark Salinas, Natalie Rodriguez Jansorn, Frances L. van Voorhis, et al. 2018. *School, Family, and Community Partnerships: Your Handbook for Action.* 4th ed. Thousand Oaks, CA: Corwin Press.

Every Student Succeeds Act. 2015. Public Law No. 114-95.

Federal Interagency Forum on Child and Family Statistics. 2021. *America's Children: Key National Indicators of Well-Being.* Washington, DC: US Government Printing Office.

Friedman, Susan, Brian L. Wright, Marie L. Masterson, Barbara Willer, and Sue Bredekamp. 2021. *Developmentally Appropriate Practice in Early Childhood Programs Serving Children from Birth through Age 8.* Washington, DC: NAEYC.

Gilliam, Walter S., Angela N. Maupin, Chin R. Reyes, Maria Accavitti, and Frederick Shic. 2016. *Do Early Educators' Implicit Biases Regarding Sex and Race Relate to Behavior Expectations and Recommendations of*

Preschool Expulsions and Suspensions? A Research Study Brief. New Haven, CT: Yale University Child Study Center.

Individuals with Disabilities Education Act. 2004. Public Law No. 108-446 and 632, 118 Stat. 2744, Part C, Early Intervention, and Part B, Preschool Education.

Institute of Education Sciences. 2022. *Report on the Condition of Education 2022.* Washington, DC: US Department of Education.

Iruka, Iheoma U., Stephanie M. Curenton, Tonia R. Durden, and Kerry-Ann Escayg. 2020. *Don't Look Away: Embracing Anti-Bias Classrooms.* Lewisville, NC: Gryphon House.

Jenkins, Jade Marcus, Jennifer K. Duer, and Maia Connors. 2021. "Who Participates in Quality Rating and Improvement Systems?" *Early Childhood Research Quarterly* 54 (1): 219–27.

Keyser, Janis. 2017. *From Parents to Partners: Building a Family-Centered Early Childhood Program.* 2nd ed. St. Paul, MN: Redleaf Press.

Kurcinka, Mary. 2015. *Raising Your Spirited Child: A Guide for Parents Whose Child Is More Intense, Sensitive, Perceptive, Persistent, and Energetic.* 3rd ed. New York: William Morrow.

Mancilla, Lorena, and Patricia Blanco. 2022. "Engaging in Reciprocal Partnerships with Families and Fostering Community Connections." In *Developmentally Appropriate Practice in Early Childhood Programs: Serving Children from Birth through Age 8.* 4th ed. Washington, DC: NAEYC.

Melton, Gary B., Susan P. Limber, and Terri L. Teague. 1999. "Changing Schools for Changing Families." In *The Transition to Kindergarten,* eds. Robert C. Pianta and Martha J. Cox, 3–12. Baltimore: Paul H. Brookes.

Miller, Edward, and Joan Almon. 2009. *Crisis in the Kindergarten: Why Children Need to Play in School.* College Park, MD: Alliance for Childhood.

Minnesota Department of Education. 2017. *Early Childhood Indicators of Progress: Minnesota's Early Learning Standards, Birth to Kindergarten.* Minneapolis, MN: Minnesota Department of Education.

Mooney, Carol Garhart. 2013. *Theories of Childhood: An Introduction to Dewey, Montessori, Erikson, Piaget, and Vygotsky.* St. Paul, MN: Redleaf Press.

NAEYC (National Association for the Education of Young Children). 2019. *Advancing Equity in Early Childhood Education.* Position statement. Washington, DC: NAEYC.

———. 2020a. *Developmentally Appropriate Practice.* Position statement. Washington, DC: NAEYC.

———. 2020b. *Unifying Framework for the Early Childhood Profession.* Washington, DC: NAEYC.

NCPFCE (National Center on Parent, Family, and Community Engagement). 2013. *Family Engagement and School Readiness.* Understanding Family Engagement Outcomes: Research to Practice Series. Cambridge, MA: NCPFCE.

Neuman, Susan B., Carol Copple, and Sue Bredekamp. 1999. *Learning to Read and Write: Developmentally Appropriate Practices for Young Children.* Washington, DC: NAEYC.

Nicholson, Julie, Linda Perez, and Julie Kurtz. 2019. *Trauma-Informed Practices for Early Childhood Educators: Relationship-Based Approaches that Support Healing and Build Resilience in Young Children.* New York: Routledge, Taylor & Francis.

NIEER (National Institute for Early Education Research). 2021. *The State of Preschool 2021: State Preschool Yearbook.* New Brunswick, NJ: NIEER.

Passe, Angèle Sancho. 2013. *I'm Going to Kindergarten!* St. Paul, MN: Redleaf Press.

———. 2020. *Creating Diversity-Rich Environments for Young Children.* St. Paul, MN: Redleaf Press.

———. 2021. "How Early Education Can Grow after the Pandemic." *Famly* (blog). August 4, 2021. www.famly.co/blog/post-traumatic-growth-early -education.

Puerling, Brian. 2018. *Teaching in the Digital Age for Preschool and Kindergarten: Enhancing Curriculum with Technology.* St. Paul, MN: Redleaf Press.

Schmitt, Sara A., James A. Elicker, David J. Purpura, Robert J. Duncan, Katrina L. Schmerold, Adassa Budrevich, Lindsey M. Bryant, and Jennifer K. Finders. 2023. "The Effects of a High Quality State-Run Preschool Program as Rated by a Quality Rating and Improvement System on Children's School Readiness." *Early Childhood Research Quarterly* 62 (1): 89–101.

Shore, Rima. 1998. *Ready Schools: A Report of the Goal I Ready Schools Resource Group.* Washington, DC: National Education Goals Panel.

Slate, Joseph, and Ashley Wolff. 1996. *Miss Bindergarten Gets Ready for Kindergarten.* New York: Puffin Books.

Smythe-Leistico, Ken. 2012. "A New Approach to Transitions: Welcoming Families and Their Ideas into Kindergarten Early Learning Setting." *Family Involvement Network of Educators (FINE) Newsletter* 4 (1).

Snow, Catherine E., M. Susan Burns, and Peg Griffin, eds. 1998. *Preventing Reading Difficulties in Young Children.* Washington, DC: National Academies Press.

Statista. "Total Number of Children Enrolled in Pre-Kindergarten Programs in the United States in 2020, by State." Accessed January 20, 2023. www .statista.com/statistics/315100/total-number-of-us-children-enrolled-in -pre-k-by-state.

Stipek, Deborah, Doug Clements, Cynthia Coburn, Megan Franke, and Dale Farran. 2017. "PK–3: What Does It Mean for Instruction?" *Social Policy Report* 32 (2).

Tabors, Patton O. 2008. *One Child, Two Languages: A Guide for Early Childhood Educators of Children Learning English as a Second Language.* 2nd ed. Baltimore: Paul H. Brookes.

Tabors, Patton O., Diane E. Beals, and Zehava O. Weizman. 2001. "'You Know What Oxygen Is?': Learning New Words at Home." In *Beginning Literacy with Language: Young Children Learning at Home and School*, eds. David K. Dickinson and Patton O. Tabors. Baltimore: Paul H. Brookes.

US Department of Health and Human Services. 2018. *Head Start Parent, Family, and Community Engagement Framework.* Washington, DC: US Department of Health and Human Services.

Vitiello, Virginia E., Daphna Bassok, Bridget K. Hamre, Daniel Player, and Amanda P. Williford. 2018. "Measuring the Quality of Teacher–Child Interactions at Scale: Comparing Research-Based and State Observation Approaches." *Early Childhood Research Quarterly* 44 (3), 161–69.

Vitiello, Virginia E., Tutrang Nguyen, Erik Ruzek, Robert C. Pianta, and Jessica Vick Whittaker. 2022. "Differences between Pre-K and Kindergarten Classroom Experiences: Do They Predict Children's Social-Emotional Skills and Self-Regulation across the Transition to Kindergarten?" *Early Childhood Research Quarterly* 59 (2): 287–99.

Zosh, Jennifer M., Caroline Goudreau, Roberta Michnick Golinkoff, and Kathy Hirsh-Pasek. 2022. "The Power of Playful Learning in the Early Childhood Setting." In *Developmentally Appropriate Practice in Early Childhood Programs: Serving Children from Birth through Age 8.* 4th ed. Washington, DC: NAEYC.